The Year of the Moon Goose:

Essays and Tidbits from the Banks of Marsh Creek

T.W. Burger

DEDICATION

To Sue, where all of my words finally fail me.

CONTENTS

ACKNOWLEDGMENTS

Oh, boy, where to start? With Sue, of course, my partner, inspiration and conscience for many years. To my brother, David George Burger, whom I admire more than I can say, and to my aunt, Shirley Miller McDonald, who is the best of all of us. To my good friend Karen Steinrock, who persisted in nagging me to get my rear in gear and put this book together and volunteered to work her marketing magic with it if I did. There are others, of course, too numerous to mention, but I will take a stab at it: The late theologian and fellow poet Roger Carstensen Sr. Th.D., who finally convinced me to write something in prose; Carol Kefalas, who persuaded me to stop driving trucks for a living and try writing; Robert Bigham, James A. Kalbaugh and Robert "B.J." Small, who launched me on a nearly 30-year-and-counting career as a journalist, to a number of editors and publishers who put up with me, some more willingly than others; for Alan and Candy Paulson, who saved my life long ago; to the Sunday Morning Breakfast Consortium, (currently Barbara Williams, Sal & Gail Prezioso, Cookie Driscoll, Mike McMasters, Dave and Wendy Slaybaugh, and assorted guests and camp followers, along with the staff and management of Café St. Amand in Gettysburg,) for their forbearance, encouragement and dark roast coffee; to Nat Frazer, John Messeder, Ira Meistrich, D.B. Frank and Jack Marlando, not necessarily in that order, who had more to do with me writing this book than they probably know, and to my neighbors on Marsh Creek Heights Road, who unknowingly loaned me their home turf as a subject and laboratory. I should also mention my garden, which served both as inspiration and suffered from neglect as I worked on this manuscript, and to the various pests that had free rein in that same garden because I was too busy to turn my attention to them I warn: I am done now. Run for your lives!

<u>Say Hello</u>

This is not a book that will teach you how to garden, or fish, for that matter.

If you are worried about thrips and nematodes or where best to plant your okra, or how to hook a prize bass, you will not find a lot of help in these pages.

On the other hand, if you want to discover Moon Goose crying on the water at midnight, and that it is perfectly all right to let your imagination come along on a year in one ordinary man's garden on a hill above a creek full of music and wonder, well, this might be just the book for you.

I would like to invite you over for a visit. Put on some old clothes and a hat to keep the sun out of your eyes.

A note of clarification: This book's beginnings lie in columns, stories, and journal entries from several newspapers and other media over a number of years. They are strung together chronologically by month, but not by year. Therefore, if in one day I speak of drought and in the next of a flood, it does not mean I have lost my mind. I lost my mind long ago when a nightmare crawled out of a dragonfly's head, but that is another story.

I wanted to start my tale with winter, because that season is the most remarkable to me, given that I grew up in the Deep South, where winter is a dank, miserable, half-hearted thing with temperatures in the 30s for the most part, and a lot of rain. I feel colder in Southern winters than I do in the winters of Pennsylvania. Here it gets cold enough for the water to freeze out of the air.

There is also the sense of starting from a dead stop. Winter seems dead for some, though it really is anything but. It is a huge coiled spring of life just waiting to crack through the ice and take off, and the marsh stoneflies come out, and our snowdrops, winter aconite and lesser celandine are suddenly up and blooming.

My garden lies on a ridge above Marsh Creek, just to the south of the town of Gettysburg. The creek snakes through some of the country's most historic ground, then makes its way south and east to join with other creeks and trickles to become the Monocacy and then the Potomac.

I do not write much about the Battle of Gettysburg that took place here all those years ago, though it permeates everything. Maybe that is why.

It is not that I do not think about the battle. I discovered a few years ago that I had cousins who charged across that heartbreaking ground with Pickett. When I drive through the Park where that fight happened, I feel differently than I did before I knew about the role of the Burger boys from Fincastle, Va.

They were grandsons of Heinrich Burger, who was a Hessian soldier whose prince rented his unit to King George. When the war was over, Heinrich stayed behind. He lived for a time somewhere a few miles to the west of the then-new town of Harrisburg, and then moved with the family he would eventually marry into down the great valley to Botetourt County in Virginia, where he farmed and began peppering the landscape with progeny.

However, I still do not write much about the battle, even though Union troops camped right here where I live. One neighbor who owns a metal detector comes up with the occasional buckle or Minié ball.

The garden is another thing. The time I spend when I am not writing for a living I like to spend in the garden. The garden is where I keep in touch with the basic rhythm, with the beat that was here before us and will surely outlast us.

My neighbors sometimes see me standing in the garden, leaning on a hoe and staring at nothing. It is not what they think. Well, not usually. I am writing, or thinking about writing. Trust me; it is harder than it looks.

My home is a little frame house on a high bank perhaps 20 feet above the creek. The house is one of a group of weekend get-away houses built in the 1920s and 1930s by assorted businesspersons, doctors and attorneys as a place to get them and their families away from the swelter of town in the days before air-conditioning. I like to say that it was Gettysburg's Riviera.

At one time, the neighborhood, called Marsh Creek Heights, was full of kids, who swam and fished in the creek, and played cutthroat baseball in the field across the creek. This was no simple sand lot, but a prepared field with grandstand and bleachers. Neighbor Dan said you used to be able to stand a dime up on edge between the blades of grass; the field was that smooth.

The field has gone to weed, and the amenities are simply gone. The owner mows it once a year, probably because of township regulations. As I write this, the only man-made things in the field are a picnic table, a bright pink ice-chest, and a red pickup truck stuck in the mud roughly at the position of shortstop.

My house sits upstream from an ancient dam, built to power a mill long since gone. The creek here is maybe 100 feet wide, and usually tranquil. The dam is a "low-head," structure, meaning that it is less than six-feet high. The state, for a number of reasons, is slowly working its way around to removing all the low-head dams in the state. There has been a dam here since as early as 1817, depending on who you ask. The dam, with some tweaks over the years, remains sound, but it really is an unnatural barrier. Even so, I hope I am gone before they get around to removing this one.

From my deck, I can watch the carp patrol when the sun is still in the east. Later in the day, the creek throws back only sky, and there is no telling what is going on down there. I cannot stay away. It calls to me with its fogs and fumes, its shimmering stillness, roiling floods, and with its giant carp lurking, bronze blimps just under the surface or churning with crazy passion during the mating season.

The creek throws up a smorgasbord of sounds. The whine of the four-lane highway more than a mile away rolls upstream when the wind is from the east. On still nights, you can hear the rasp of the little green heron, and in the heat of the day the croak of the great blue, the caws of crows, cries of osprey and red-tail hawks, and the splash of carp throwing themselves out of the water during their rut.

We begin, then, in winter, when everything is cold, and seems dead. But we know better...

T.W. Burger,

On Marsh Creek,

Gettysburg, Pennsylvania,

Autumn, 2012

Marsh Creek from the deck, mid-Winter

WINTER

"One [practitioner of science] is the educated man who still has a controlled sense of wonder before the universal mystery, whether it hides in a snail's eye or within the light that impinges on that delicate organ." **Loren Eiseley**

December 21, Solstice & Daffodils

Here it is, the death of the world.

That is what we used to think, anyway, a long time ago. If you do not pay attention, it does seem like everything is dead right about now.

Sometime around noon, the tilt and whirl of the earth in its long dance around the sun conspired to make this the shortest day and longest night of the year.

The winter solstice.

The sun went down at its furthest point to the south this evening, behind an old wreck of a barn on the other side of the fifty-acre field beyond my garden.

Now, we are on a three-month voyage to the equinox, when the day and night stand eye-to-eye,

Winter Solstice

And so it goes. Three months past the equinox will come the summer solstice, when the pendulum has reached the opposite side of its arc, and the sun goes to sleep at the far end of that same field, past the burn pile and the beds for the homeless daffodils. It will be the longest day of the year, and shortest night.

Tick, Tock. Always and forever, or as much of always and forever as we are going to get.

As clockworks go, it is reliable, but it does need resetting now and again.

That explains Leap Year, the one year out of every four when we add a day just to keep everything adjusted to our calendars and all these artificial structures we've tacked onto the real world as a way of laying claim to it, the way the colonial Spaniards poked flag staffs into an endless series of beaches and claiming everything in the name of their king, while the natives stared out from the underbrush wondering.

The daffodils are not homeless, of course. I mean, there they are, plainly in residence.

My partner Sue is nuts for them, as was her mother before her. Polly even had a variety of miniature daffodil named after her.

When we combined households many years ago, we ended up with a lot more daffodils than we knew what to do with. There are only so many corners that need filling. We corralled them in some of the raised beds back in the vegetable garden, where they pop up every spring.

They do not hang around for long. A friend, Richard Ezell, who is sort of a wheel in the daffodil world, said growing daffodils consists of 50 weeks of hard work and two weeks of bitter disappointment.

Yes, there is a daffodil world, and wheels within it. They have national and international conventions. I have been to a couple of them, though I am more of an idle onlooker than an expert.

There is a big difference. I like to see daffodils shoving the frozen dirt aside as winter dwindles. It is a comfort to crunch through the garden on the way to the burn pile on this solstice day and to think of them a few inches below the surface, life coiled and ready for its time to come around again. Therefore, I like them, smile about them when I walk by, but I do not know their names.

A true daffodil lover does, though, and can point out every flaw on every bloom at a flower show. I am not sure I want to know something well enough to be able to see what is wrong with it from 10 feet away.

My first daffodil society convention I sat in on a seminar on daffodil genetics. I am not kidding. I realized that I was sitting in a room with people who knew there are 20,000+ varieties of daffodils. And care.

Late in the night, I heard the Moon Goose honking out in the yard. He is a lone domestic goose that hangs around this stretch of the creek. He is as white as the full moon, and cannot fly, for some reason. We gave him that name because of the way he seems to glow in the light of the moon. He has discovered that if he hangs around our back yard long enough, we will spot him and toss him some corn. Who would ever guess that a bird would understand Pavlovian conditioning?

We began to feed him during the deepest snow, when it seemed evident that he was going hungry. He has since come to expect it, and will stand there and yell his head off until we toss something down. Now and then, I will take corn or bread down and stand there while he eats. If I get too close, he hisses and calls me foul names. Or fowl names. Ingrate.

Christmas: Big Tree, Big Heart

I am sitting here in a comfortable chair with my feet stacked up, all laid-back and comfy, laptop teetering on what remains of my lap, and a mug of hot tea perched nearby. I am thinking about my father.

Standing at the other end of the room is the eastern red cedar we just murdered out in a farm field and mounted on the sill of the bay window.

My father has been dead for more than a quarter-century, but now and then I see him in the mirror, lurking in the bones of my face, or sometimes he kind of floats up unbidden from something I hear or see. This is one of the latter.

You do not usually find eastern red cedars on the Christmas-tree lots or at the "cut-your-own" farms because, for one thing, they're as common as fleas, they're really prickly, and they do not smell as good as some of the higher-grade commercial trees.

If I had to be pinned down to describe the odor, I would say its bouquet is piney with a soupçon of cat pee. But then again, it was free.

My perception of the smell may, of course, be simply prejudiced by my intense dislike for Christmas. Before you ask, I do not know why. I just do. However, hating it is cheaper than liking it, and takes less time.

The placing of a tree is only a big deal inasmuch as it is the first I have had in my own residence in 30 years. Sue said she would really like one this year and so now we have one.

Cutting the annual Christmas tree was always a big production for Dad. I think he took me and my brother along every year when he went to go get one. Sometimes we would go to a lot, but the clearest memories are of hiking out into the Georgia piney woods somewhere, cutting down a tree and lashing it to the Dodge for the drive home.

My father was not an emotive man. He often sat by himself, smoking his Viceroys and staring at some memory or another.

However, some sort of largesse overtook him when it was time to get a Christmas tree. You would have thought he was selecting one for display at the governor's mansion. Yet I do not think we ever got one that did not need major surgery before we could even get it through the door.

It was sort of a family joke.

I remember one year, in a riot of excess, Dad took me and David and his bow saw out into the woods to look for "just the right tree." I do not know about David, but by the time we found this blessed conifer, I thought we had walked all the way to Colorado. It was getting dark, and the tree seemed enormous.

"Gee, it looks, um, big," I think I told him.

"It is fine," he said. "It is just right. We do not want a tree that's too small."

Not a problem, as it turned out. It took forever to drag it to the station wagon and strap it to the top. When he saw how it dwarfed even the 1958 Dodge, a vehicle roughly the size and maneuverability of a minesweeper, I think Dad was beginning to think that maybe he had gone a little overboard.

I am not saying it was big, but the car looked like a bedroom slipper on which someone had perched a watermelon. It was a really BIG tree.

At home, Mom took one look at it and went to sit in the family room.

The tree would not even go through the door until Dad trussed it up with some clothesline. Then, when he tried to stand it up, he got it to about 45 degrees and the top hit the ceiling.

Out came the saw, and the clippers.

He sawed, pruned, and tried again. Still too tall. And again.

Ditto.

The third time did it. There it stood, massive, occupying a third of the living room. The Tree.

Well, not so much a tree, as a green furry cylinder. Dad had to trim it from both ends, so that by the time he got it upright and bolted into the holder, what we really had was just the center of the pine tree. It seemed to rise out of the floor and go straight up into the ceiling. No cone-shape for the Burger household, no sir. We had us an evergreen silo.

Fortunately, we did not have much furniture. There would not have been any room for it.

It was splendid, once we got all the lights and ornaments, fake snow and phony icicles on it. I took to sleeping on the floor in front of it until Dad would come and more or less drag my sleepy butt back to my bedroom. I loved that tree.

So, today, a little reluctantly, I dragged my Grinch-y self out to that field, selected a cedar, and sawed it off at ground level. I selected a short one, because it was going to stand on that windowsill. I stood in front of it and checked out where the top of it came to, just a little above my eye level.

I maneuvered it through the house and laid it in front of the window where it will stand through the holidays. I looked at the window. I looked at the tree. I looked back at the window.

I distinctly heard my late father say, "It is just right. We do not want a tree that's too small."

It must be something genetic. I dragged the tree out to the deck, sawed 8 inches off the trunk, trimmed another 10 or so off the top, and used the clippers to bring it back to something like a taper. Then I carried it carefully back through the house and set it on the sill.

Perfect.

Frogs Again.

I approached the long, skinny Christmas gift from Sue's sister Wendy with some trepidation.

After all, One Never Knows.

I remembered a previous Christmas when I opened an oddly shaped present from Wendy and discovered therein what I still refer to as the Fabulous Flying Frog Birdhouse. It is about the size of a small toaster-oven, made of an indescribably green plastic. From its front and back legs, which are moveable, and from its little froggy butt sprout bright green feathers. On one side of the grinning frog is a circular hole a little more than an inch across, with a stick protruding beneath it.

It was pretty awesome.

This spring and summer, it lived sitting on the porch outside the bedroom, high on a plant shelf among the begonias.

There were plenty of birds around, but none built their nest in it. It may be that the birds in our neighborhood are too conservative to live in a frog.

I wrote a column about the FFFB, and actually had a woman in the Midwest contact me and ask me where she could find one just like it. She just HAD to have one.

The frog itself came from China, for "Pacific Rim...The Company for All Seasons." The company, based in Seattle, went bust in 2007. Therefore, my

FFFB is probably now a collector's item and worth tons of money. So there.

Let me make it plain. We do not collect frogs. We HAVE a collection of frogs. We picked up a couple of fiberglass frogs for the garden, just for fun. Then we picked up one or two more. I am not sure why. In addition, a couple of friends, seeing a frog here or there, bestowed more upon us. But we do not actively collect frogs. We just have them.

That said, there I was, on the evening of Christmas Day, and I had another gift from Wendy sitting in my lap, wrapped in happy green paper.

A box, maybe six inches by two inches and two feet long. What could it be?

I shook it. A kind of clanking, with a hint of a ringing. Hmm. Bells? A wind-chime? An Erector Set? A do-it-yourself, easy-to-assemble Honda Asimo robot?

Gingerly, I tugged the ribbon loose, shredded the paper away, and cut the tape sealing one end of the box.

Holding my hand out, I dumped the box's content.

Frogs.

Again.

Note the plural.

FLYING Frogs.

Again.

Three of'em. Happy, goofy little fellers, pounded out of copper, I think, about six inches long, with butterfly-like wings, and attached to the end of a long metal rod, so I can stick them into the dirt so they'll appear to be flitting about in my garden.

But we do not collect frogs. Please.

A Tithe of Foxes

Christmas Day, time on my hands, I took a walk to the old iron bridge on Cunningham Road. It is a mile or so from my house, uphill and down, and a walk seemed a good way to shake off the holiday cobwebs.

The day was one of those winter partly-cloudies, when dark, brooding cloud masses share the perfect blue sky with blinding sunlight. From the high ground, I could see the rolling fields giving way in the distance to the dark, knotted Blue Ridge Mountains.

As far as I could see, the inky clouds parted, now here, now there, allowing sunlight to lance down, highlighting now this field, now that copse of trees, and now a white house, which lit up against the background gloom like a lamp.

As a boy, I used to think those rent places in the clouds were windows into heaven, and if I looked hard enough, I could see angels, standing around the rim, keeping an eye on things.

When one is young, heaven seems within reach.

I always wondered what God and his gang thought of the airliners passing through their domain.

Down the long hill to the bridge I trudged, listening to the water trickle down both sides of the road. I remember when I first moved here how I marveled at how it seemed every hillside seemed to have a wealth of springs. Everywhere I looked, water seeped from cracks and hollows. I once dreamed that I lived on one side of a vast earthen dam that was beginning to fail.

The bridge itself is one of those iron truss bridges built a century and more ago. It has been out of commission for a while, after somebody fell asleep at the wheel and punched out one of the abutments. The bridge, too narrow for modern emergency equipment, will one day be replaced with one of those characterless reinforced concrete bridges.

I like to go there and stand, listening to the endless chant of the water. In warm weather, if one is still, one can see muskrats playing in the shallows, and deer coming down to drink. Even when the Cunningham Road Bridge was open, it was possible to park in the middle of the span and watch the creek for 10 or 20 minutes before someone else wanted to cross the creek.

But the road is only a mile or two from one of the intersections with the four-lane road to Baltimore and Washington, D.C., and the zoning hereabouts is very friendly to developers. Visiting the bridge and its rural surroundings is like going to see a sick friend who is not expected to get well.

My mood at the bridge was more somber that I would have wanted Christmas to be. The muskrats had gone to wherever muskrats go in the winter, and the water was high, murky and turbulent from the previous night's rain.

On the bank at the foot of the bridge were the skinned carcasses of four foxes and the forelegs of a deer, arrayed at the edge of the rising waters like some primitive sacrifice, to whom or what I do not want to guess.

It was not a sight I cared for on Christmas Day. I turned and headed back up the long hill toward home. On the way, the fickle sun lit a stand of red-tipped trees against the blackness. The trees flickered like flame, or rising lightning. Overhead, the sun picked out the white belly of a hawk. I zipped up my jacket, for the wind had picked up. Above, heaven receded ever further away.

JANUARY

Ghosts in the River

Three days before the year's end, and the weather had turned suddenly colder.

Scattered fat snowflakes darted through the scrub oaks clinging to the steep banks of the Shenango River in western Pennsylvania, a 100-mile long tributary of the Beaver that eventually flows into the Mississippi River.

Shenango means "Pretty One."

My brother David and I joked that if we believed in ghosts, we could imagine our mother's would be down there on the marshes along the Pretty One, gigging frogs with her dad, a rough, hard-drinking steelworker.

At our feet, on the heights above the river, were the headstones of our mother and father. Dad was buried there in 1981, Mom about 30 years later.

Neither of their lives or deaths was particularly easy. But all that is done, now.

Water, flowing water, has always held me fascinated. I grew up in northeast Georgia, along the Oconee, whose name is a corruption of the Creek word meaning "Born From Water."

The Oconee's waters tumble down over the fall line to join the Ocmulgee to become the Altamaha and finally meld with the Atlantic.

I now live in southern Pennsylvania along Marsh Creek, which joins with Rock Creek to become the Monocacy, which flows into the Potomac. The word Monocacy means either "River with Many Bends," or "Well-fenced Garden," depending on whom you ask.

The heights between Marsh and Rock creeks were the site of the Battle of Gettysburg. Bullets and other martial debris show up in the farm field behind our house.

The thing about rivers and creeks is that they seem from moment to moment to be fixtures, but in truth, they are never the same. Blink and you missed something, something that will find its way to the eternal time-sink of the sea. They are at once symbols of opportunities lost and of hope. That is how I think of it, anyway.

David still lives a short walk from Born From Water.

We do not get here often. It is a long haul for me, and a longer one for him. Visits to our mother's sister bring us back, and we always make the trek to Riverside Cemetery. I do not know how often we would get back if not for her.

This is our first trip back since Mom's ashes were interred over Dad's grave.

I will not speak for David, but I usually spend an hour or so sitting on Grandpa George's headstone, gazing over the tops of my parents' stones, down toward the river.

I am not there for them. There is nothing beneath the assorted Burger and Miller stones but organic debris and the odd discarded mechanical part, here a bone, there a set of dentures.

I go to address memories, good, bad, indifferent, sometimes surprising, things I had forgotten. I speak, sometimes aloud, about this or that. Long ago, there was not a little anger, as I worked through things as I aged.

I am in my sixties now. The anger is gone, dispersed by understanding, nubbed by weariness, and sometimes dimmed by no longer giving a damn. They were ordinary people, as am I, flawed, beaten down and badgered by their own past. As am I. Who am I to be angry?

I leaned against the big oak above the graves. The wind picked up and the flakes came more heavily.

In a few weeks, The Pretty One will be frozen over. In the old days, there were spots where you could drive a car over it. In recent decades, the winters have been thinner, meaner, somehow.

David and I climbed back into the car and wove our way through the smoke-blackened gothic stones and back into the end-of-the-year bustle of town, leaving The Pretty One counting down the moments to spring.

Bee in Winter

There I was, just a week into the New Year, staring at a honeybee.

Unusually warm weather for south-central Pennsylvania had brought her out to bump and buzz, bewildered, looking for blooms that are still months away.

I wonder where her hive is. Bees typically forage up to two miles from their hives if food is plentiful, and up to six if it is not.

It is just barely warm enough, at 55, for her to be out.

Her abdomen pumps in and out like an accordion. She is breathing so hard I imagine I hear her puffing as she rests there on the table by the creek, her wings tattered lace. I expect she is near the end of her short life.

There is no pollen held between her back legs. There is no pollen to be had. I prop my head on my hand, watch as she catches her breath, and try not to be overwhelmed by the futility of the whole exercise. Poor little clockwork. I doubt she will see the spring. It is possible she could live her entire life without ever seeing a flower.

I take note of her stinger, poised over the glass surface of the table. A marvel that such a small thing, that sting, can bring a much larger creature – me, for instance – to such singular attention. She will not use it, the experts say, unless provoked or threatened. I intend to do neither, and so am not very worried.

Only the female bees have stingers, and that is all I will say about that.

Suddenly, her accordion still playing a polka, she lifts off from the table, angles sharply up to the roofline, then weaves her way through the tangle of winter-bare branches, steadily in search of something bright and sweet and life-renewing, something that is not there and she will not live to see.

I guess it is a kind of Faith.

The Song of the Ice.

We just came through an ice storm. Black ice shimmers on the roads and on the walk to the house. Light glitters off the new ice on the creek, the open water widening and narrowing as the temperatures fiddle around trying to decide if they are going to get serious about this whole winter thing.

I miss the singing of the ice.

My first winter here on the creek, it froze over solid. The neighborhood cats used it as a way to get to the other side and tear into the population of voles, mice, and squirrels. The ice got to a foot or more thick. I have been living north of the Mason-Dixon Line for going on 30 years. I am still astonished by ice.

I grew up in the Deep South, a place that taught me many things. One of those things I learned as a small boy was that Jesus was the only one who could walk on water.

Up here, in those years when winter gets serious about its work, you can drive right over the top of your favorite lake, chop out a hole a foot or two across, and go fishing, with your car or truck sitting patiently suspended over groggy game fish and slumbering snapping turtles.

I once went to cover an iceboat race for a newspaper. I wound up standing about 100 feet off shore, fidgeting awkwardly about 100 feet from the bottom. I never did relax.

It did not help that I am also afraid of heights.

Back here at the creek, the singing riveted me. As the water beneath the ice rose and fell, the ice cracked lengthwise, up and downstream. The creek bed amplified the sound, and the song in the snow-stilled nights rose up, haunted, hissing, humming, the twang of a hammered saw, whisper of arrows flying, the snap of whips.

The first time I heard it my hackles rose, not knowing what it was. Even after I understood, nights when I would stand by the creek in the moonlight and listen, I would wonder if that, indeed, was all the answer. It had voice, and a hint of song to it, and I would catch myself trying to understand the words.

Over the past decade or so, the winters have warmed and become more erratic, the bone-aching cold punctuated by periods of mild temperature, so that the ice falters and never finds its voice. The long nights are poorer for it, though we still find the occasional midnight with the ice-encrusted trees glittering under a robust moon, the breeze filling the air with the sound of ten thousand tiny bells.

Maybe the song has stilled because of climate change. Maybe it is just a cyclical thing, and next year, or the next, or the one after that, the ice and music will return, and I will stand by the creek under the moon once again and hear the song of the ice whip back and forth in the silvered light.

For now, the creek is silent, and all I can hear in the depth of the night is the trucks on the highway, a mile or two downstream. It is a poor substitute.

I stood creek-side just after sunup this morning watching geese feeding in the shallows near the opposite bank. Ice crinkled the surface, thin and mostly transparent, revealing the rocks and weeds beneath.

It has been years since we had a long, hard winter, with ice thick enough to drive a car on, and snow so deep that the creek seems a wide white road through a forest. I do not miss the heating bills, but I do miss the sounds of a deep winter night, where the tree branches clatter in random percussion. A still winter night is so quiet that the silence itself is almost a sound.

The Garden Nailed in Place

The garden lies still, locked in snow, transfixed by the stems of dead weeds and mummified sunflower stalks.

I do not know which is harder to believe, my memories of how the same space of ground teemed with life only a few months ago, or the idea that it will be again. Today, it seemed as likely to burst into bloom as a slab of pig iron.

When I worked away from home, I had a 50-mile commute to the newsroom. I spent a lot of time hyperventilating and thinking of new adjectives to describe drivers who think their 4x4 vehicles are immune to the laws of physics.

Crawling down the roadway at 20 or 30 miles an hour slower than usual, I began to notice things I had passed way too fast in good weather.

How, for example, the occasional flare of sunlight shoving its way past the cloud cover throws the shadow of a wooden fence across the roadway, leaving a bold pattern down the length of the pale pavement.

How the ice clings to the hunched shoulders of a looming Santa Gertrudis bull as he stands in a rugged pasture, a teak-colored mass of meat, king of his little hill.

More observant than I might otherwise have been, I noticed today while helping a friend feed and water her two dogs how very different water looks in a snow-whitened world, poured from a bucket in light robbed of reflections from grass and flowers.

The husky, an idiot bundle of fur with egg-white eyes, refused to take shelter, even in a fall of freezing rain. He hopped and wriggled in his run, his long outer fur pearled with ice.

A Pupsicle.

The Doberman, more focused, plowed through the snow, head down, sniffing out voles, tail a mad metronome.

Back home, I stood in the failing light, listening to sleet falling over the yard and garden, a sound somewhere between a tick and a hiss.

The snow cover has melted and refrozen into a kind of meringue. It snares great hunks of the winter sunsets and holds them shimmering under the bare trees.

One of the blessings hidden in the folds of winter storms are the seed catalogues.

Naturally, the new seed catalogues came during one of the busiest weeks I have had in a while, and I have had no chance to go through them. They just sit on the coffee table, giving me the printed equivalent of a "come hither" look and waiting for that dark afternoon when winter seems it will last forever.

I am not there yet. I am still rather enjoying all this. However, the day will come when shovelling the walk and feeling the car fishtail have lost their novelty. On that day, I will spread open the catalogues with their bright photos of plants, prettier than any I have ever grown, open a sketchbook and begin to conjure up a new garden.

January 15, Fantasy Gardening

The thing I hate about gardening magazines is that they explode with photos of gardens owned by people who obviously have a lot of spare time and money. Many of them seem to have the equivalent of a Ph.D. in garden science. Or lots of hired help.

I am not sure anybody would buy it, but I wish there was a magazine about the gardens the rest of us tend. Or fail to tend, for that matter.

I am a regular guy, with no special gift for growing things other than tear-thumb weed, tree-of-heaven and common morning glory. Outside of the mental, spiritual and physical benefits of the activity, my garden experience goes in three phases:

The dream garden, in which the beautifully photographed flowers and veggies in the catalogues and magazines transmogrify to the garden of my imagination. That garden's soil is easy to dig, a sandy loam of magical properties. In this garden, my flowers are bright and brave, my tomatoes a comic-book red, the size of cantaloupes, and ecstatically delicious.

Reality sets in when I realize that the handicapped sticker hanging in the windshield of my car means more than I have trouble walking and climbing stairs. It means that digging and bending over are a lot harder than they used to be. It also means that the geometrically straight rows accomplished in the magazine either by an out-of-work MIT graduate or through the magic of Photoshop. By the end of planting, I am sticking in seeds and starts at random.

In addition, there is the matter of my winter-made promises to keep everything in the garden tidied up and organized, not a weed anywhere, every tomato and pepper getting the maximum nourishment. Daily routines falter, attention wanders, and by midsummer, the garden looks a little down-market, shabby, like an old pair of shoes with the toes curled up.

Harvest always brings the guilt of all the things I could have done better. It is a lot like real life, only faster. In the end, what ends up heading for the kitchen is not as pretty as the stuff in the magazines, but it is mine. I guess that is a lot like real life, too.

In the clean up after harvest, I promise myself that I will do a lot better next season. This has been true every autumn for nearly two decades. It has never turned out to be true, really. This, too, could be a kind of Faith

Forgiving the Mouse

The little bastard looked right peaceful, smooth slate-gray fur, tiny ears, soft as velvet, his eyes closed. He lay curled on top of the mysterious box of wires that told the furnace what to do and when.

Notice the use of the past tense.

He was dead as a box of rocks.

Long ago, I did some reading about modern scientific thinking and theories and all that. Most of it was way over my head. I remember feeling something like vertigo when I tried to wrap my mind around what they call quantum physics, which is complicated enough that one scientist said, "Anybody who says they understand quantum physics doesn't understand quantum physics."

Anyway, one of the things I read had to do with the interconnectedness of things, and the consequences thereof. It went something like "a butterfly fanning its wings in this country sets off a chain of events that result in a typhoon in Burma," or words to that effect.

Being a simple soul, my first thought was that it must have been a very LARGE butterfly.

Did I mention that I did not do all that well in the part of science that required logical thinking? Never mind. Logical thinking probably would not help with quantum mechanics.

Well, the late field mouse on the box in the basement has a lot to answer for.

Do not get me wrong. I confess that I rather like rodents. I once lived in a mobile home set on the edge of a cornfield in a windy valley, a place where the winter blasts would sometimes pluck bits and pieces off the structure, and send them sailing toward New England. Sometimes the wind twisted the trailer enough that the hanging lamps would sway.

My only company was my cat, Phyllis Killer, and any number of field mice who would risk Phyllis' appetite and prowess to come in from the corn for a little warmth and food.

I was not a very good housekeeper. At night, sitting at the table writing, I would watch as the little fellas would slip out of hiding and nibble on macaroni noodles I had left on the counter during one of my minimalist post-dinner cleanups.

The mice would sit upright, nibbling away and watching me with their bright little button eyes.

Obviously, I was single during this time.

Stop cringing. The mobile home was out in the middle of nowhere and I enjoyed the company. Besides, any creature courageous enough to nibble macaroni only a few feet away from Phyllis earned every noodle.

Back to the rodent curled in state atop the box next to the furnace.

He was dead because he had been chewing on things in the old farmhouse Sue's family owns a few miles from our place.

Rodents do that because their front teeth never stop growing, and they have to chew constantly so that the incisors will not grow overlong to the point that they do not allow the beast to eat.

Everything went fine for the little guy until he started chewing on one of the wires coming out of the box. His teeth met on the 24-volt copper wire. It arced and popped apart and the mouse died.

Now, think of that butterfly, flapping up a typhoon in Burma.

If I understood what the plumber said, the wire of the mouse's demise ran from the control box through the walls to the vacant upstairs apartment in the old farmhouse. The thermostat, set as low as it would go to keep pipes from freezing, was no longer able to send instructions to the furnace.

The temperatures plummeted into the single digits. The pipes in the baseboard heaters froze, and one burst. Then, in a day or two, the temperatures climbed above freezing.

The pipes thawed.

Hot water, pushed by the pumps elsewhere in the system, spread out over the floor, steaming in the frigid air. The smoke detectors identified the steam as smoke and signalled the alarm company that the 200-year-old farmhouse was on fire. By the time we got there, three fire trucks had arrived, and a small tribe of volunteer fire fighters.

The fire fighters made sure there was nothing actually on fire and left us to our chores. A couple hours of wet-vac and mopping – and a visit from the plumber – later, and the place was in a condition where the only thing to do was keep the heat on and fans running in hopes to keep down the amount of stuff that needed to be replaced.

And put out some tempting, tasty poison in the furnace room.

Sorry fellas.

Worthy of Weasels

"It is not what you look at that matters, it is what you see." **H.D. Thoreau**

On a warm September afternoon on Little Cumberland Island on the Georgia coast a scientist and I walked along the two tracks of what passed for a road. I was interviewing him about sea turtles, his particular area of expertise.

"There!" he exclaimed every few feet. Bending over, he would pick something up and show it to me; another serrated black triangle, a fossilized shark tooth.

We walked about half a mile, all told. When we were done, he had a whole pocketful of shark teeth.

I had none.

No matter how much I squinted and cursed, I never saw a one on my own.

The scientist, Dan Stoneburner, got a good laugh out of it. He gave me one of the teeth, to remind me that looking and seeing are not the same things.

We like to think they are. We pretend that the signals sent flashing down our optic nerves to our brains are somehow the sum total of the world as it is.

Actually, given the limitations of our equipment, we only see a narrow slice of the various wavelengths of light out there. We will never know what the world really looks like. It is as though we were born in a barrel, and forced to make sense of it all from what we can see through the bunghole.

Worse, it is not as though we use even this limited equipment to its full advantage. The "wiring" from eye to mind varies widely from one individual to the other. Hence the shark teeth invisible to me that must have seemed to flash in neon to Stoneburner.

And so it goes with me and weasels.

I am told by people who are supposed to know these things that this area along Marsh Creek is simply teeming with weasels. To hear them talk, I should be tripping over them.

I have lived here nearly 20 years and have never seen one weasel, discounting a few encountered during elections, when one rejects the lesser of two weasels.

Sorry. Where was I?

I can only assume that either the entire weasel population has been wiped out by some plague, or through some strange alchemy of inattention, I simply do not see them.

It cannot be the weasels' fault. I cannot imagine them crouching behind tree trunks, snickering among themselves as I pass by, visually weasel-less.

It must be me. I just do not see weasels.

I cannot complain too much. Here at the creek I have seen snow geese, tundra swans, muskrats, blue herons, white egrets, bald eagles, osprey, deer, bats, snakes and snapping turtles. I hope one day to see a golden eagle, since we are very near their migratory flight path.

In other places, I have seen bears and wildcats, raccoons, opossums, moose, elk, water moccasins as big around as my arm, alligators, and bison. I once found myself face-to-face with a mama bobcat whose cliff-side den I happened upon while climbing the cliff. Fortunately, I was not very far up.

I have even ridden an elephant, but that is another story. Critter-wise, I have been blessed.

But I have never seen a weasel.

Perhaps I am not worthy. Perhaps I should read everything I can about weasels, study their diet, their mating habits, and learn where they prefer to live. Maybe it is simply a matter of paying my dues.

If I do all that, maybe one fine summer day I will be slipping quietly along the edge of a cornfield, or along the banks of the stream. Something will catch my eye, some shift of the slanting afternoon sunlight. I will move, quietly, slowly, to the side of a large rock. Parting the fronds of a tall fern, I will see it, sitting motionless behind a small grouping of stones and a piece of stump, a perfectly formed and flawless shark's tooth.

But still no weasel.

FEBRUARY

Notes: Snowmobiles and Land Tides

1. The face of the creek changes constantly. In fact, the only thing constant here is change itself. All summer long, we watched as various birds and plants began to make their homes in a large uprooted oak tree that had become jammed on the rocks during the spring floods. Last Friday we had some warm weather and torrential rains. I left the house for a few hours. When I returned, the four inches of ice and snow that had carpeted the creek's surface for weeks was gone. So had the oak tree. We searched downstream as far as we could see. Even with binoculars, we could find no trace of the oak. It was as though it had never existed.

2. One new thing turned up, however. Down at the dam, we discovered that my neighbor's jon boat had slipped its moorings and become entangled with some trees and blocks of ice the size of automobiles. It looked like a little tin toy some child had stomped in a tantrum.

3. I talked to a scientist who told me about land and air tides. It is not only the oceans affected by the pull of the moon. He said in the six hours or so it takes the full moon to pass over the North American continent, the entire land mass rises a foot and falls back.

4. The atmosphere, too, heaves moonward, as though reaching out to snare it. These phenomena were first discovered and recorded after we started measuring the earth from satellites. My dreams

flickered with visions of the earth heaving under the moon, like a great beast deeply sleeping. The phrase "solid ground" will never mean what it used to.

5. My friend Hugh told me yesterday that the winter up where he lives has been really severe.

"We got lots of snow," he said. "More than anybody remembers seeing before." In fact, there was so much snow, he said, that a friend of his had gotten a snowmobile for his wife."

I remarked that it seemed like a very thoughtful thing for his neighbor to do.

"Yes," said Hugh. "I do not know what she thought about it, but he thought it was a heck of a good trade."

Do not feel bad; I walked right into it, too.

Moongazing I

Before going to bed at night, I often stand on the deck for a while. I usually say I am "looking at the creek," but that is an over-simplification.

I am looking at the creek and the moon, at the calligraphy of the tree shadows on the layer of new ice formed after the previous layer was swept away in a flood last month, and at the array of colors glinting off the million facets of the snow, light that arrowed out from the sun 93 million miles away, careened off the rough round face of the moon, ricocheted off the ice crystals, fractured into rainbow hues and collected into my own two wondering eyes.

It still has the energy to startle.

I listen to the wind in the trees and the muttering of the geese on the peninsula upstream, the banshee moan of traffic on the highway a mile to the south, to the hooting of owls, the complaint of the Moon Goose, and the singing of the ice.

Let us not forget the stars. I lived in town for a long time, where the stars hid behind the glare of streetlights. These winter nights, I am re-learning the constellations: Orion, the Dippers, and a few others.

It will take time. It is obvious, I told myself the other night as I stared at the stars trying to remember names, that I have spent too much time looking down at my feet while wonder spun madly overhead.

If a superstitious person happened to see me from across the creek on a cold winter night, I am sure to give them a start. To keep warm on these frigid nights, I sometimes wear a heavy wool garment given to me by a friend.

It is the outer wool robe, or jalabiah, worn by men in Middle Eastern countries to fend off the chill evening air. Pulled on over thermals and a sweat suit, it keeps me warm in 20-degree weather, even for extended periods.

I was on the deck last night, talking to a friend over my cell. The robe, essentially black, is nearly floor-length, and comes with a very deep hood, which I had pulled over my head for protection against the wind.

I had a sudden mental image of someone on the other side of the creek looking over here to see the Grim Reaper, standing on my deck, talking on the telephone.

That person might think my number was up. But I feel OK, thank you very much.

<u>Moongazing II</u>

Just before sleep, I stood looking out through the windows, at the snow-packed trees outlined starkly, gracefully, against the slate-dark creek, chalky calligraphy from some lost language.

The moonlight illuminated the flying air through the clouds. There were no shadows. Everything seemed lit from within.

Snow at night makes me think of absent friends, of old songs, of bright windows and dark woods, a fire, and a big dog at my feet.

My heart prowls a vast wilderness, where the dogs of my youth still run; Gramps, with his bark like an old man griping. Faithful, goofy Pooch, and Rascal, who never realized he was, in fact, big in heart only.

I wonder again how to describe the sound of snow falling. It is not so much a sound as flecks of silence.

As promised, the snow had started in the early afternoon, a few flakes at first, almost an illusion, and a dream.

Within the quarter-hour, snow had gauzed the big cedar across the road, and the east bank of the creek faded to a dream.

It snowed all day and into the night, thick and heavy, without a breath of wind.

It lay along every branch and twig, on every stubborn brown leaf on the pin oak, and mittened the seed clusters on the weeds by the garden path. Fence posts marched their way across the bright fields, wearing top hats of snow, and the little concrete Buddha at the base of the silver maple was suddenly Santa.

In the morning, the creek reflected the vague sun snared in the branches of the creek-side oaks. I bent to the task of shovelling walks, envying a friend who owns big, furry, galumphing dogs, the kind of dogs that make a walk in snowy woods worthwhile. I looked at the cats, who stared morosely at the snow that makes their bellies cold and wet. Cats are fine, but there is something about a dog, a big, rowdy, grinning, antic, redneck fur ball in the depth of winter.

I stretched my aching back, bent again to the path. The groundhog has said there will be six more weeks of winter.

If I had a dog, I would teach him to hunt groundhogs.

By the time the walkways were done, the wind had picked up. The trees shrugged off their shrouds. The drowned sun made its getaway from its oaken tangle, and I stowed the shovel, kicked off the snow boots, and went in to make some tea. The cats, with no visible sign of gratitude, used the newly cleared paths to patrol their territory, bellies dry, tails high

A Long Walk Between Seasons

5:11 p.m.: As I write this, snow flurries again swirl in the failing light between here and the ridge opposite.

I walked this afternoon down along my side of the creek to the dam, past what the January flood left of my neighbor's Jon boat and then through some scrubland, just to see what was there.

It had been one of those days when it is evident great things are afoot. The wind blustered, and the temperatures that had climbed into the 50s began to fall.

There remains about the day a feeling of purpose. The sky passes by overhead, ever changing and in a hurry, as though undecided what to wear, first partly cloudy blue-and-white, then a sombre dark gray. It is as though the weather cannot make up its mind whether to go to a picnic or a funeral.

A shower of rain fell, very briefly, then turned to ice pellets, then to snow, and then stopped, all within about 10 minutes.

Crows filled the air with derision. The roar of the wind in the leafless webbing of the trees blended seamlessly into the sound of snowmelt rushing over the dam.

Beneath the dam on the southern banks of the creek stands a wilderness of trash trees and briars, with dark sepulchral cedars scattered around, sentinels with nothing to guard.

Two Canada geese launched themselves into the air from upstream. Three more joined them in a few seconds, rowing for altitude as they disappeared down the long, crooked valley of the creek, into the uncertain sky, heading for their roosting spot. Moon Goose flapped his wings, honked, but remained stuck in the rabble of shallows and boulders where an island once stood.

The woods had grown dark, and I was suddenly aware that my aged boots were no longer waterproof. I jammed my notebook back into my coat pocket and trudged through the briars toward the road, watching the geese angle into the fading west, envious as I labored through the mud and tangles, wheezing with effort.

Fog

A little after one a.m.: The sounds of rushing water fill the night, and I suspect that once again all the ice has swept from the creek in the heavy rains. I turned on the back floodlight, but the beam from the lamp dashed itself to pieces among a billion fog droplets wrapping the world in dirty cotton.

The fog itself was almost warm, and brushed against my exposed cheek like damp satin, a sensation sensual and uneasy, necrophilic.

The frightening and enticing thing about fog is its quality of hiding. We do not fear that we may step off something, or run into something we already know. Rather our fear and our secret hope is that the things we know may really be illusion, and that anything, anything at all could be going on just beyond our blunted sight, just out of earshot, our worldly senses hoodwinked just long enough for legions of the dead or squadrons of angels to pass by on unspeakable errands, mute and secret.

Barefoot in February

The past few weeks we have had these spells of spring weather, as though the season had taken an earlier flight and gotten here sooner than expected, and had then gone back south for another week or so.

Earlier today, I stood on my deck in my bare feet, drinking coffee and watching the local wildfowl. Nice, of course, but very hard to bear when Old Man Winter sneaks up and blind-sides us again, which he will.

I try not to read too much into the weather. Global warming/climate change is a fact, naysayers to the contrary, but the kinds of swings we see are within the normal range. I checked, and the array of record highs and lows for the past week or two run from 11 below zero to 75 above. As a meteorologist once told me, any kind of weather can happen any time, and that is that. Weather and climate are related, but not the same.

Wooly Bears, Whistle Pigs, etc.

Just as naturally, we have had a spate of spring-like weather. You know, the kind of weather that in September or October we would have called cold and wintry, but in February seems balmy. Just as the catalogues arrived, it snowed, and the temperatures started falling.

It was just a little while ago that the media were full of the various and contradictory predictions made by assorted groundhogs around the country, chubby rodents that either did or did not see their shadows, indicating that we will or will not have another six weeks of winter.

I wonder who it was who first had the idea that in terms of seasonal prognostication we should follow the predictions of a tubby rodent. Other than TV weather forecasters.

With all their computers and satellites, these folks cannot seem to stop talking about weather predictions by groundhogs, woolly bear caterpillars, and other nonsense.

One of the newspapers where I used to work posted this on their website recently: "If the woolly worms are correct, schoolchildren might be getting a number of snow days this winter," the story's lede read.

Truth be told, I think the paper runs this story, or a version of it, every year. I can attest to that because I wrote a couple of them. Over the years, I have written my share of weather stories, and stories like those of woolly bear caterpillars and other arcane folk methods of predicting the weather.

I would be willing to bet that every news organization in the U.S., if not the world, is writing stories on the same old humbug every year. It is a journalistic tradition. Not necessarily a good or useful tradition, or even really journalism, but a tradition nonetheless.

Weather stories fall into two main categories.

The first are the ones I am talking about here, where some group of local experts or shamans or hoodoo doctors picks some innocent critter, like the caterpillar or groundhog, and bases some prognostications about what the weather is going to do in the coming weeks or months.

The groundhog, or woodchuck or whistle pig is a marmot, one of a variety, unbelievably, of squirrel. Why anyone ever thought groundhogs could predict weather is a mystery. However, the caterpillar's reputation as a forecaster is even more mysterious. The groundhog looks at least vaguely like us, like a fat gnome in a fur coat.

The caterpillar, well, it is a bug. It is covered with black or dark brown fuzz with a band of orange or light brown fuzz in the middle. Supposedly, the more black fuzz there is, the harsher the winter will be.

My guess is that the reason we attribute the ability to predict the weather to a larva is part of an effort to pretend that the world is really all about humans and their comfort and well-being.

I have to admit, it is a tempting world-view. It would be nice if some thoughtful designer had set these things out for the truly wise so they would know how cold they were going to be.

Sorry. The amount of black on the thing depends on how far along it is toward being full-grown. The older the caterpillar is the blacker he is.

The only thing the caterpillar knows, if caterpillars can be said to know anything, is that when it gets cold he goes to sleep and wakes up in the spring as an Isabella tiger moth. Whether this state of affairs is alarming to the former caterpillar is not known.

The second type of weather news story includes the ones where the reporter spends an hour or so writing a story about how it snowed, so that his readers can shovel their way out through the snow to their newspaper tube and read about it.

In my view, this explains a lot about the decline in print media. Most of us just look out the window.

Unlike the first category of weather story, however, this one can actually be very useful, because the reporter can link in helpful information such as when the local snowplows can be expected or, with today's budget cuts, if they can be expected, and whether or not there are school closings. Most parents pray that there are not, I do not care what they say in public.

I have a friend who worked for a regional almanac for a number of years. I met him when I did a story on how his weather predictions, using all sorts of odd calculations based on a formula put together hundreds of years ago, had hit every major winter storm on the nose.

Caterpillar readers everywhere nodded sagely. See? Those scientists do not know everything.

Well, actually, my friend IS a scientist, in fact, in the fields of math and computer science. The almanac stuff was more of a hobby, like tying flies. That year, by the way, was the only one in a very long while that his predictions had any accuracy to speak of.

You are Here

It had been a long walk in the muck, on legs that had spent too much time tucked under a computer table. In addition, I will completely deny any suggestion that I might have been for a brief time lost. I knew where I was all along. All I had to do was look down, and there I was.

I will admit, however, that for a few minutes I was not entirely certain about the location of anywhere else.

Finally, the thicket in which I had been entangled opened up, and I recognized the cornfield around which I had trudged confidently an hour or so earlier. Up the hill, I could make out the row of wobbly garages lining the old farm road on which my house sits.

Home. At last.

This place, this little corner of the world felt like home in a larger sense from the very first. I moved here from the place I had lived for 30 years, and never once felt a twinge of homesickness.

This must be where I am s'posed to be.

Not long ago I took a break from some of the remarkable adventures that arise from home ownership and took a long ride. If you are not from here, the specific names will not mean a lot to you, but they should give you a feel for the remoteness of the places they indicate:

I gassed up in Waynesboro, and then took 997 to Mt. Alto and 233 through the rucks and rumples of

South Mountain to Caledonia, thence up the ridge nearly to Ironmaster's Forge, then 234 to the very top of the Blue Ridge. Determined to stay off the beaten path, I jammed and slammed down what could be called a road only if one were feeling generous.

I spotted a fire tower, and parked the car to go have a look. I did not see any No Trespassing signs but then, I did not look very hard.

I tried hard not to remember that I am afraid of heights. Rubbery of knee, I managed to make it all the way up to the trap door in the bottom of the shed at the top. I was tempted to go in, but I spied a gray box fastened to the underside that clearly contained electronic gear, which I supposed could easily include an alarm system, and so thought better of it.

So, plan B: Just stand on the little platform and have a look-see.

Obviously, the tower was not for public use. Picture a post-card with a railing and you will have a pretty good idea what it was like. It would have taken very little bad luck for a person to stumble and bang his or her way through the steel grid work to the ground, a queasy distance below.

Still, by gripping the angled steel frame, I could look out over the tops of the trees and see forever.

Looking west, the muscular ridges on the far side of the Cumberland Valley stood out in bold relief in the late afternoon sunshine. Closer, the valley itself lay, strewn liberally with farm silos and fields peppered with cattle.

My paternal ancestor had travelled down that valley to Virginia in the late 1700s. To the northeast, the mountains marched, and I believe I could almost make out Dillsburg, perched on the very end of the Blue Ridge. To the east, after searching for it just a bit, I made out Big Round Top on the Gettysburg battlefield and very near my house. A little further, on, I am almost sure, I could make out the Pigeon Hills, more than 30 miles away.

Suddenly, it all felt like home, cozy and near, and like a piece of a vast puzzle, very much itself, and yet an undeniable portion of the whole.

I was reminded of those T-shirts and posters depicting an image of the Milky Way galaxy with a little arrow leading to a tiny spot at one edge, the label reading, "You are here."

And so I was. For a moment, I could almost make out the arrow.

In my mind's eye, I saw my little corner of creation radiating out from that tower, the valleys just so, the hills here and also there, laced by the filigree of innumerable hillside seeps, springs, and creeks, along a bend in one of which stands this cottage where I live and write.

All the whole of that fits just exactly into the pieces of the puzzle adjoining it, which forms a gas-shrouded ball - our local neighborhood planet - which whirls around a rather average sun, which itself is part of that greater dance around the galactic center, the whole shebang heading off in a great rush of 50,000 mph or so toward, I think, the Horsehead nebula.

I felt as though I should fasten my seatbelt.

Dizzy from all that movement, I stood there long enough to see the eastern flanks of the far ridges fade to blue. I practically had to pry my fingers from the angle iron before making my cautious way back to the ground.

Not long after my adventure on the fire tower, I called a fellow from one of the more western communities in our county as a source for a story.

He wanted to know why a reporter from the newspaper in a town at the base of those Pigeon Hills was calling him. I had a brief temptation to tell him we were all passengers on the same ride, whirling out through the universe on the fringes of a flaming spiral galaxy. but thought better of it.

Snapshot

The geese are almost constant companions here on Marsh Creek. The wide, still spot on the creek, just above an ancient dam, is a social center for the geese. They sail in here about dusk, honking and carrying on like dowagers at the world's largest church social.

Each goose tries to maintain a larger territorial domain than it is capable of managing. Each makes a great deal of noise, moves a lot of air and water with its wings, and generally keeps things stirred up.

Later, when the geese have gone, the creek remains much as it ever was.

There is a lesson there, somewhere.

Fog II

On an ordinary sunny day, a walk in the woods is a jumble of images, rocks, creek, trees, and, in their season, ferns, flowers, bugs, birds, all in one big visual jumble.

Not in the fog. Then, everything is shrouded and mysterious, tucked into gray. Things present themselves in discrete clusters, forcing me to look exactly THERE, where the trunk of a cedar so green it seems black shoves against a lichen-speckled piece of limestone the size of a horse's head.

Or THERE, where a tangle of honeysuckle, pin oak, and a blushing briar vine tell you that even in the fog, winter is hardly as dank and gray as you expect it to be.

North side of the Garden, December

Poem

St. Valentine's Day.
Funny to both of us,
Raised in warmer climates,
That this day should be so wintry.
Near four feet of snow in the last week, they say,
And more coming, they say.
Yesterday, the sun so bright on the pristine fields
It was hard to look, though I did, arriving at work
Dazzled.
The best thing about snow is
The sound cars make when they drive through
When it has just fallen.
Tires in
Confectioners' sugar.
I like it less after it has packed, become
Inflexible, brittle, frail.
The older I get, the less I want
To be reminded of
Frailty.
But then I think down,
Down beneath the cracked, pocked cover
To the quiet dark where your bulbs slumber,
Dreaming of their perpetual
Surprise.

T.W. Burger

Kitten Kaboodle: Staying in the Moment

Outside, trees and shrubs tugged at their moorings. In a riot of branches and pinecones, it seemed as though they really wanted to get away in a hurry.

It was a weekend after a bad week, one of missteps and worries. Now the sky had gone from gray to black. Wind howled and hurled things at the house. Rain hissed on glass.

There was not a lot of rain, but the wind bulled its way up from Texas and other rowdy areas in a way that indicated what it thought of Yankee landscapes.

The kitten, Kaboodle, purred like a Cummins diesel and chewed on my hand.

She was naked.

Kaboodle is one of the semi-feral cats that live outside, bumming around on the deck, and living on handouts. We have an ongoing project to spay and neuter the population. It could be going better. Hence, Kaboodle, and Autumn and Agate and Amber, and a few more.

Kaboodle was inside because she came down with some bacterial equivalent of the Mongol horde and was clearly dying. We scooped her up and took her to see Doc Dodson. After a couple of weeks of dosing with medications and special food, she was bouncing off the walls and full of mischief.

She was also, as I noted, naked as a new bird, and warm as a fresh biscuit.

Well, nearly naked. She is normally a longhaired cat, but her feeble condition left her disinterested in personal hygiene. By the time we intervened, her coat was a filthy mass of felt, impenetrable, a nasty amalgam of fur and feces.

There was nothing to do but to have it all clipped off, and keep her inside until the weather warms up and she has some protection. By that time, of course, she will be part of the household and probably never be an outside cat again.

I have to say that there was not a lot of cat under all that fur. The groomer clipped off everything but the fuzz around her face, the end of her tail, and her feet. She looked like a rat in a lion costume and fuzzy slippers.

Outside, the wind was hitting gusts of up to 60 mph. Now and then, something thumped against the wall, as though the wind were hurling small children at the house. With each strike, Kaboodle turned toward the source of the sound, and stopped purring for perhaps a full second.

I leaned back in the recliner, watching the front move through, clawing at the world as it passed by. I played with Kaboodle, who returned the favor, and at the same time tried to show me how to live in the moment.

Poem: Six

Today I saw that the first
Snowdrops have awakened,
Pushing aside the
Dark tangle of soil.
Sly green tongues
Whisper of a riotous spring.

T.W. Burger

Liar Liar

The weather report is a lie. As I read in the living room just a little while ago, the wind smote this little house as though it had given offense, angry paragraphs of rain hissing at the windows. Moon Goose complained from the creek, making a sound I could imagine coming from a soggy bassoon.

Doug Allen, the TV weather guy, said there would be "showers." Maybe some wind.

The sky to the east sounds like a violent argument that has moved away, but still within earshot. In the trees a constant roaring dwells, a sound I can easily imagine resides forever in the minds of psychotics, hemmed and defiant in their institutions.

It is nothing personal. Nature rages because that is what Nature sometimes does. The best we can do is to try to stay out of the way, like puppies in the presence of rowdy children.

I feel like writing Doug a little note, telling him that he ought to move some of those computers and scanners off to one side and put in a damn window.

Keeping an Eye on Davey Crockett

Winter is not giving up without a fight, but the end, literally, is foreordained. The seasonal waltz around the sun says that the equinox is soon upon us. The signs have been with us for some weeks now, growing stronger over time, as might a crescendo in some great symphony.

The maple in the front yard has put out buds, as have the twigs on the assorted tangle of botanical riff-raff along the creek below the dam. Daffodils shove their way through the mulch around the oaks.

In the past few days, I have watched as one of the neighborhood beavers tugged a branch toward his burrow in the northern bank, and two kinds of mergansers rested in the creek on their way back north from their winter nesting grounds. Best of all, I saw two large flocks of snow geese, at least 30 in each formation.

Among all these other signs of spring, I must include the sight of a neighbor boy, stalking along the creek-side, BB-gun at the ready. I stood at the window, watchful, remembering my own adventures with my faithful Daisy Model 25.

The more I remembered, the closer I watched. A thriving population of free-lance cats has not been of any great benefit to the songbird community here, and the last thing they need is a budding Davey Crockett in their midst.

I know this from experience, haunted as I am by the ghosts of innumerable small beasts whose only sin was holding still for too long, and in range.

Actually, it has not been such a good winter for the outside cats. They tend to collect around my house because the former owner, a sweet little old lady who looked to be the prototype used to design the first grandmother, made me promise to take care of them.

My care has extended only to feeding them table scraps and some inexpensive dried cat food. Over the winter, a few of them began to look a little the worse for wear. By the end of February, some had disappeared entirely.

One of the missing was my personal favorite, a scrappy little tom I called Cappy, because of the little black "beret" perched jauntily on his head.

Cappy was not any bigger than a New York minute, but he was not one to back down. The local thug cat, a bruiser of a tom with the unlikely name of Butterscotch, drops by regularly just to show everybody who is boss.

The thug usually left Cappy pretty well shredded. The last time I saw him, I think he was more hole than cat.

Nevertheless, life goes on. Yesterday as I was out receiving a raft of verbal abuse from Moon Goose for not being quicker at getting him his corn, I noticed that the female cat I call Peaches seems to be getting a little wide in the beam.

Looks like I will not have to worry about running out of cats. The birds will just have to take their chances. I will do what I can. I will keep the bird feeders up high.

In addition, I will keep my eye on Davey.

Snapshots II

1. The last few days sparkled with a kind of magic. The late afternoon skies have been generally clear and filled with flocks of snow geese and other wildfowl returning north from their winter sojourn in the south.

Activity is highest along the creek here at sunup and again at dusk. Today I spotted for the second time a beaver busy with his errands on the east side of the stream. This morning two pair of wood ducks fed just beneath my office window.

2. I still have not seen any of the herons that haunted this place until late fall. I think of the heron as sort of the totem animal of this house, because the first day we saw the place, wondering whether to make an offer, a heron flew by over the creek at eye-level and made up my mind for me.

Now you must excuse me, for Moon Goose kvetches.

Onion Snow

A light rain falls, the cold, listless, weary rain of winter near its end. It is a hunch-over-when-you-walk, raw rain.

The little police scanner in my office spits out the recorded NOAA forecast with mindless repetition:

"Winter storm warning southern half late tonight and Thursday for possible snow accumulations of six to 10 inches. Snow spreading from south to north tonight. Lows in the mid 20s to low 30s...."

The scanner hisses and pops, as though trying to provide a soundtrack for the scene outside the window.

"The reason for the warnings and watches is a low pressure system over eastern Kentucky. Unlike storms this winter season that have moved northwest.... "

Beyond the window, the flakes swirl and loop against the dark trees across the creek. How can the forecasters sound so calm, I wonder.

I picture a giant force rising over the winter-dark mountains of Kentucky, bending the steely air to its will, wrestling it out over the heaving shores to spawn more of its kind as the salt spume whips and the beaches sigh.

In the diner this morning, a cheery, wide woman shivered in from the sugary outside air, brushing at the coarse cloth of her coat.

"It is the onion snow," she said.

Maybe, I thought, too wary of the weather to hold it to a commitment. The onion snow, the gardeners tell me, is the last one of the season, so named because it usually comes after they have their onions planted.

The seasons are always running to catch up to the round rush of the world. In late December, the northern hemisphere leaned once more toward the sun and summer. The belated airs playing over the beaches of Rio eventually took notice and began their northward mosey, shoving at the heavy, cold winds from the north, as they do now, playing hugely over the knobbed and glittering eastern U.S.

They never really quite get caught up. In high summer, the dour cold air masses of the north will still be squabbling over turf with the sweaty southern air when the sun starts its long stalk toward winter.

Meanwhile, down here in the realm of smaller forces, things go on much as before under the steady glow of the streetlights. Trucks on the four-lane a mile or so downstream growl as they hit the hill on this side of the creek.

Midnight. Another circle begun as the sun sweeps toward dawn.

I reach to turn out the light. The Peterbilts, Macks, and Freightliners wink out into the dark hills, jewels falling into ink.

The onion snow shifts and swirls onto the ordered and stirring fields.

Pants on Fire

I set myself on fire today.

It was quite accidental. No heroic self-immolation in protest over whatever for me, nossir.

When botanist and dedicated gardener Liberty Hyde Bailey died in the 1950s, friends and relatives going through his belongings found that the handle of his garden hoe had grooves in it from many decades of his grasp.

Sadly, my work ethic is not that intense. For example, I spent the afternoon clearing the dead plant material from the garden in order to plant Brussels sprouts and red-leaf lettuce.

What could POSSIBLY go wrong?

But I used fire to burn all the dead stuff away, balling up old newspapers, placing them on the windward side of the rows or the mass of old tomato vines, and lighting them up.

What could possibly go wrong?

In my defense, I can say that I have used the method for years, and never had a fire get away from me, at least as far as the area of the garden goes. I always stand there the whole time clutching the garden hose.

I clear out quite a lot of ground this way. The trouble was, this time, that I kept daydreaming as I walked around, stomping on fire that had wandered into places where it should not have been.

I had just extinguished some flames in a particular spot and had begun daydreaming about some raised beds I wanted to build when I discovered that my feet and lower legs felt uncomfortably warm. The reason for this was clear: I was wearing an old baggy set of Army fatigue trousers, several inches too long and very ragged.

At the moment, they were on fire.

Not wishing to appear nonplussed by such trivia – staying cool is also a guy thing -- I moseyed over to the water hose and extinguished myself. Well, it was an energetic mosey.

"Gee," I said, or words to that effect, "I thought these pants were flame retardant."

Then I realized that it was not the pants that were retarded.

I think it is time to wear some grooves in my hoe.

It is Time

Gardening is an instrument of grace. **May Sarton**

Spring is here, officially, but it does not seem to want a big deal made about it. The temperature today crept up to 45 and gave up, and the wind made the temperature seem 15 degrees cooler. The clouds remained high and curdled, though we had no rain or snow.

Still, Easter eggs and candy festoon bare dogwoods in the suburbs.

The days suddenly seem almost long enough. The road home after work is no longer a drive through a tunnel of darkness.

Soon, people on the streets will forego their bulky winter wear and start to look human instead of so much dirty pastry.

It is a time to forget to take home the jacket you wore to work in the chill morning because the afternoon is so warm.

This weekend churches will bloom with children decked out in new outfits, the little girls budding out in flouncy dresses, a mobile bouquet in a riot of colors.

Along the drive through the woods to the house, under the winter-browned riot of honeysuckle and tear-thumb vine, regiments of daffodil leaves, muster for the first assault of the new season.

Spring on Marsh Creek

Soon, the dark ground will crumble and heave out new growth of every sort, from early flowers to the first clacking, leggy hordes of bugs that make a gardener's life so full and varied.

It will not be long before wood and thicket rustle with the annual commotion of new birds and baby rabbits, a fact the cats already seem to anticipate: They seem more watchful of late.

In the muddy pond bottoms frogs begin to stir, as do turtles, which have spent their winter buried in mud and breathing through their butts, something I prefer not to think about too much.

One wonders, maybe, what would that be like, what would one dream in the oozy dark while winter locked the pond overhead under a cracking, singing roof of ice?

It is time to start scanning the wintry gray flanks of South Mountain, looking for that first hint of green, for the first startling lavender of the redbuds. Before you know it, a green cloud of leaves will hide the stony bones of the ridges, the outlines of the hills, and the fat, high houses of rich showoffs cluttering the ancient hills with matchstick arrogance.

Anglers will finger eagerly through their tackle boxes, dreaming perhaps that this year the cold lightning trout will not be so fast or so wary. Perhaps, they dream ahead even further, to the lunker bass lurking in the lakes and ponds of summer.

Along the creek, I keep watch for the scattering of blue herons who make life for the frogs and fish interesting, if shorter. Maybe, with luck, ospreys, or even a bald eagle, will again hang out in the dead oaks across the water from the house.

I predict that soon there will be afternoons when it will be necessary for me to take my laptop out to the deck, or to one of the local parks, because whatever story I am writing will somehow need the touch of sun on shoulder, and the sight of children teeming around playground equipment like so many brightly colored birds on a trellis.

There is no help for it. It is not my fault.

Love at First Sight.

There is no other way to explain it. This is roughly the anniversary of the day we first spotted this house after driving down a gravel road we had never been down before. In fact, we had thought it might be a driveway.

We had been looking at houses for about six months. It had not been a very happy experience. I was fond of telling people I had found one I could afford, but there was a robin living in it.

The problem is not that there were not any houses available. All those pesky people from Maryland and D.C. who have more money than sense have been coming up here willing to give twice as much for a house than most people would. The owner of one house I eventually lost to some big-pockets was insulted by my offer.

"Do you know what this house would bring in Baltimore?" he told my Realtor and friend, the late Tom Phillips.

"So, tell him to take it to Baltimore and sell it," I snapped.

Poor Tom. A number of those gray hairs on his head were likely my fault. Some of the missing ones as well.

We looked at everything, including a vinyl-clad log cabin in which there was only one room where I could stand upright, and another house with a great view, right through the walls.

Then we saw the place. It was on a gravel road I had not even known existed, along a creek. It was not even on the market, technically, but I had heard that it had been, but nobody had made any offers, so it was delisted.

I called the owner. She knew who I was, and invited us over for a look.

We walked through the kitchen and dining room and onto the back porch and looked over the back yard, which is mostly Marsh Creek.

A blue heron croaked and flew by slowly at eye-level.

"This is it," I thought.

"We'll take it," I said.

"Shouldn't we look at the rest of the house?" Sue asked, her eyes wide.

"The rest of the house doesn't matter," I said.

OK, that was stupid, and I should have been a little fussier about the ancient furnace and the roof that looked like it itched, but overall, the house really was "it."

I will not describe the process it took to get the loan and go through to the actual closing. I had always been under the impression that The Inquisition was over. Silly me.

The closing itself was a real education. It was as though I had attended a parade held in my honor, complete with confetti.

My job was to sign all the confetti.

Then it was mine, and the real work started. OK, "mine" is a legal fiction. It will belong to the bank for the rest of my life, assuming I do not default on the loan or win the lottery.

There were things to be torn down, and I am good at tearing things down. There were things to be built, things to paint, a floor to replace, things for which I have no talent.

The first day, I began to think I had made a monumental mistake.

But I went and sat on the concrete wall at the creek's edge. After a few minutes a bass big enough to wear a saddle cleared the water in search of a bug, and upstream I recognized the telltale wake of a muskrat. A flight of Canada geese squabbled overhead and splashed into the darkening water downstream.

I was right, I thought. This is it.

Rain, Roses and Chili

Nothing is stranger than real life.

Home from a shopping trip, Sue and I walked around the south side of the yard. She cooed with delight to discover that several of the Lenten roses she had planted were in bloom, showing a somber tone of something like purple, like beet juice with milk in it, and a yellow center.

While I worked at bringing in the bags, Sue hurried to make a big pot of chili for dinner. That chore done, I did some straightening up in the barn, the small, enclosed space behind the garage. After half an hour or so, I trudged back to the house.

At the entryway, it hit me, the aromas from the kitchen fan pumping a glorious bouquet of onions, red bell peppers and jalapeños into the cool, dank air.

It was just a moment in time; I stood transfixed, muscles too long dormant stiff with an edge of ache in them, mind preoccupied with thoughts of flowers and vegetables wrestling up through the March mud, and then to be swarmed over by air full of sexy food smells. A moment worth holding on to.

APRIL

<u>Scouting the Spring</u>

I just got back from a whirlwind trip into the belly of the Deep South, and I can tell you that the spring that is crawling its way toward us along the ragged spine of the Blue Ridge is a fine one.

The naturalist Edwin Way Teale wrote that it takes about six weeks for spring to find its way from the Florida Everglades to the woods of northern Maine. If that is true, in driving nearly 800 miles south I moved ahead a couple of weeks into the coming season.

I drilled my way into Dixie, taking the Interstate system for the sake of time, down to the gardens of the Biltmore Estate in Asheville, and then wandered a bit in Georgia, winding up in the azalea riots of Callaway Gardens.

I returned, bearing a buckeye sapling from a nursery in Warm Springs, Georgia, and about 10 new pounds, the latter a direct result of a long-delayed reunion with southern cuisine.

Spring is coming like a green wave, frothed with a thick scattering of dogwood. As I drove south, the herringbone gray of the woods gave way to first a mist, then a fog, then a flood of new leaves. By the time I had reached central Georgia, most species of tree were in full leaf; the forests sparked liberally with dogwood, flamed with azalea, glowed with red maple.

Heading back home, it was hard, turning back toward winter. It was cold and wet up here. In Georgia, the temperatures strained toward 80 degrees. I tried not to think about the long drive back, watching the green glory turn back to gray, as I slogged north where the tracks of winter are still fresh.

The journey restored my love of the South, where I grew up. It has also reinforced a feeling I have always had, but which grows stronger with each year, with each loss. It is simply this: It is not only the spring that is fleeting. There is so much to see, so much at which to wonder. Every day, I try to remind myself: "Pay Attention!"

Epiphany, not Hooky

There was no time for it, to tell the truth. Deadlines loomed. Editors gnawed their pencils, or whatever they gnaw these days. Keyboards, maybe.

The last thing I should be doing was taking off for a ride in the country.

I had spent the morning staring at the computer screen, while outside the thermometer lolled in the 70s as a saucy spring breeze jazzed up the wind chimes outside the office.

There was nothing for it, then, but to take a trip to the post office. It is roughly six miles from here. In spring, a round trip can take hours.

I had taken a theoretical wrong turn and found myself buzzing along the Mason-Dixon Line, not even going fast enough to get into fifth gear.

Oh well.

I have learned to accept these things as they come, for epiphanies do not come to those who go out and look for them.

I am not talking about chatting up an Old Testament burning shrub or having a sudden understanding of the Unified Field Theory. I mean the small miracles that make the spin of the world more musical. Like the day I drove down a road I had been down a dozen times, only to find, this time, the roadside flamed with daffodils. Or the day I looked out my car window at a familiar pond to find, fixed in the middle like a jewel in a plain setting, a lone swan.

Or the day I went for a ride and discovered, all on the same local farm, a herd of buffalo and a herd of alpacas.

You just never know, which is exactly the point. You have to leave the door propped open, and then pretend not to watch what flits by.

I returned to the computer, feeling a little like the astronauts must feel after a week orbiting the earth. So much packed into the senses, and so difficult to share it.

Extinction by Flower

Flowers are not the first thing I think of in the spring.

Sure, I enjoy the surprise of snowdrops jumping up in the lawn, like kids having cleverly fooled the slow, dim grownups at hide-and-seek.

It is also true I enjoy standing under the pear tree on a breezy day, while its petals swirl around me, scented snow.

But I must admit that in spring I pay more attention to the woods transforming from a linear gray hash to a greening fog, and to thoughts of the garden, of the ancient alchemies of the soil.

But not so much today. Mulling over the second mug of coffee this morning, reluctant to begin another day in front of the keyboard, I considered the mass of flowers in the vase at the table's center.

It was a typical spring mix, several varieties of daffodil, with a smattering of giant snowdrops.

It has often been said that it is a shame that flowers last such a little time before they wither. Would it not be great if they could bloom all the time, some say.

Yes. And no. They would not mean the same thing if they were not so ephemeral. Somehow, flowers tough enough to last all year are hard to imagine. Delicacy is the very essence of flowers.

But then, toughness may be a matter of definition. After all, flowers may have helped bring about the end of the age of dinosaurs, or at least boosted the fortunes of their successors, a somewhat horticultural aiding and abetting.

Consider that many millions of years ago, toward the end of the rule of the giant reptiles, flowers did not exist. Plants reproduced through pollen and spores, as surviving species such as ferns and conifers do today. Plants spread slowly.

The lords of the earth, the cold-blooded Behemoths, survived by eating huge amounts of green plant material, or by eating huge helpings of dinosaurs who had eaten huge amounts of plant material.

Then, along came flowers, with their self-contained seeds, each of which contained a rich supply of food to send the new sprout well on its way.

Over a relatively short period, as such things go, flowering plants and their seeds took on a bewildering array of shapes and functions. In the grass family alone, which includes all the cereal grains that make up the bulk of our modern diet, there are more than 6,000 species.

Those little packets of food, in their uncountable varieties and numbers, made a wonderful food source for a number of to-that-point insignificant smaller creatures, including the mammals.

And, as luck would have it, something went terribly wrong for the dinosaurs. There was the matter of a very large asteroid crashing into the world in what is now the Gulf of Yucatan, causing the world to get cooler. A lot cooler. On cold nights the giant reptiles wound down like great, weary clocks

Meanwhile our warm-blooded ancestors ate seeds or other creatures fattened on seeds, and sprang about in the undergrowth. Sparks of life in the chill, they darted about the feet of the giants, warm, and busy getting smarter.

Dragon Slayer

Their warm-blooded condition meant that they had to eat, pound-for-pound, more than a reptile of comparable size. There was a trade-off, however. When the temperature dropped, those with the internal furnaces remained alert and active, ready to feed or flee, whatever the occasion demanded.

The reptiles, meanwhile, turned to zombies when their blood cooled with the air.

Therefore, maybe from now on when I head for the garden, hoe over my shoulder to wreak havoc among the weeds, I will be a little more respectful, show a little deference for the flowering ones. It is, after all, proper in the presence of something that changed forever the face of a planet, and helped defeat monsters.

Benediction

The day was perfect. In the blue sky, clouds raced dramatically, pure white on top, a glowering gray below. The pastures, brown only a few weeks ago and sugared with late snow, had erupted into the most stunning greens.

It brought to mind a day very much like it at a farm where I lived some years earlier, a few miles west of here at the foot of the Blue Ridge.

Juncos, crows, titmice dashed around full of spring errands; grackles wrestled with lengths of vine and straw for nests. In the big field, red winged blackbirds sang once again.

A brisk wind demanded light jackets as the two of us went for a late afternoon walk. The clouds, scudding in the higher winds, sent quick shadows flitting across the emerald fields, orchards and woodlots, just beginning to mist over with green buds. The patchwork fields blinked on and off, now dark, now light, as the sun and clouds conspired to highlight this aspect of the landscape and hide that, and then change the whole arrangement 'round again.

Rushing shadows and changing light put the world in a flux, which it always is, and gave the feeling that great things were happening all at once, and that was true as well.

I, for one, had been waiting for the swan.

At the same time the previous year, give or take a week or two, I had walked just at sundown to the ponds a few hundred yards down the road to think and watch the geese.

I had always thought the geese graceful, both the Canada geese and the six domestic geese from the farm down the hollow that swam among their wild cousins.

I had been watching the geese for a while when something new glided into view around a spit of land. White as a blizzard, with black legs and bill, moving among the lesser birds like a visiting king: a swan.

He made the other birds seem like students in the presence of a master.

I watched until it was too dark to see.

The swan hung around all the next day, but was gone the next morning. The pond seemed more vacant than usual.

I read that swans are sociable except in the breeding season, and that they mate for life. This one was alone. A local birder told me that he likely stopped at the same pond every year, on the way between his winter and summer homes. That is why I had been keeping an eye out for him, and got lucky again.

As the world seemed to flow along in a river of light flowing into dusk, I saw him, that unmistakable form circling over the larger of the two ponds for several breathless minutes.

Then it flew away.

I walked back to the house for supper. The first stars were out, the horizon a Mardi grass of color;

but something had gone out of it all, some benediction denied.

I tried to write about how that felt, to have gone looking for that grace and not finding it when and where it was supposed to be. That night, the writing did not go well.

Finally, I pushed myself away from the keyboard and turned off the harsh desk lamp. I drifted around, shivering a bit in the unheated room where I worked, thumbing through old books and otherwise dithering. I stopped to stretch, listening to my vertebrae popping and griping.

Idly, I glanced out the window. The ponds glowed in the twilight like jewels on ink. Gliding like an answered prayer across that bright surface the swan moved slowly, effortlessly, across the bright smear of sun colors on the black waters. Then, his wingtips writing overlapping rings on the surface, he arose, circling higher with each turn, and climbed back into the sun, amen.

Green Fog, Deer, and Flying Bass

Every year I watch closely for the arrival of spring. I like to think that, living right on the edge of a creek in the woods, I would know for sure when it arrives.

No dice. I watched the calendar. I took note of the swelling of buds on the trees, of changes in the songs of birds. Still, there came a moment when I looked out the window and realized that somehow, spring, the real thing, the ineffable moment, had slipped past me again.

Every year, I think I am going to catch that moment, the point where the seasons tilt on the fulcrum of the year and shift from winter to spring.

I am convinced there is such a place, such a point in time.

Every year I make the same promise. I will pay more attention, watch more closely, and listen for the first spring peepers.

This week the woods creek-side has lost its winter gray. A verdant mist has come drifting in, blurring the outlines of the tree trunks. The understory, a snarl of bracken tangling the forest floor, has already begun to leaf out. In a few weeks, the veil will be back in place, and the woods will once again hide secrets.

Just a day or so ago, I thought I spotted a smudge of blue against the opposite bank. In the binoculars, I could see it was a heron, a Great Blue, standing head-on, hunting for small fish in the shallows.

It has been a long time. I will have to look back through my records from last year, but I do not think we have seen any herons around here since sometime in November. My Audubon book says they winter as far away as the Galapagos and the West Indies. In addition, I spent my winter up to my asterisk in snow. So, who is the dumb animal here?

\#   I sat by the creek for a long time last Friday, when the temperature rose luxuriantly into the lower 80s. It was late afternoon and I had hit a slump in the writing and needed a break, perhaps more than I thought.

On sunny afternoons, the creek becomes a huge mirror, hiding all within it with a busy tapestry of sky. After a long, relaxing time of watching the clouds drift from bank to bank, I was just getting ready to go back in the house when a large bass leaped right out of the sky, breaking the parade of clouds into a series of blue and pewter rings.

\#   One thing I had forgotten over the winter. Traffic sounds from Route 15 fill the air, auditory smoke. It is the aural equivalent of someone burning trash upwind but far away. The smell is not pleasant, but not strong enough to complain about. It is that sort of noise, rather like distant surf, with a hint of whining.

An Eye Peeled for Wood Ducks

For Mike Hofe

A year or two ago, I was talking to my friend Mike Hofe about life out here along the creek, and about how some of the migratory birds that had disappeared in October and November seemed to be coming back.

"Yeah," he said, "You'll be seeing wood ducks any day now. Keep an eye out for'em."

I did, and two or three days later, there they were, shy and shrill and arguably one of the most beautiful waterfowl one can see.

Mike had an eye for these things, more than I ever will. He was an artist, not one educated in some academic cloister, but one who created out of a need to know, somehow, a thing that was beautiful, through and through.

Mike loved carving waterfowl, or decoys, if you will, though the ones he carved were not meant to bob around in some drafty inlet luring the real things in to their doom.

The times I visited him at the shop he and his wife ran when they were not busy being cops, he would be surrounded by carvings of birds in various stages of creation. He would show me this or that and talk about the problem of making wood take on the aspect of bird, making the static and dead vibrant and seemingly possessed of movement.

Typically, he would shrug off the difficulty with some wisecrack or another.

"It is not all that hard," I can hear him say. "You just carve away all the stuff that doesn't look like a duck."

Just this week, I watched a mallard drake preen himself on a rocky outcropping at a bend in the creek. Some of the poses the duck struck were not exactly what you would call graceful. Ducks are not very self-conscious.

Then, in one instant, and only for an instant, the drake stood, alert and erect, just so, as the afternoon sun shimmered giddily on his emerald neck. It was a moment for which there are really no words.

I wondered how Mike would have looked at that drake at that moment. Would he have taken mental notes, planning how to capture that something, whatever it was, about that moment that made it different from all the other awkward moments of the duck's grooming? Would he despair of ever finding a way to make mere wood and paint mimic that shiver of sun on gleaming feather?

Art is, finally, mute. The windy explanations of the critics at galleries and museums are just that, a wind for blowing dry leaves. In the end, I do not think there are words that can explain art. If there were, why ever bother? Decades ago, someone asked the famous dancer Isadora Duncan what one of her dances meant.

Exasperated, she said something like, "If I could say it in words, why dance it?"

Just now I had a vision of Mike, listening to me go on like this. He would flick an ash off his cigarette and look at me over the tops of his spectacles. Then he would say something impolite. He would probably be right.

He was right about the wood ducks, too. They were there, just as he said they would be, and every bit as beautiful.

They are gone, now. They hung around for a week or two, and then moved on, possibly heading further north for the summer.

Mike is gone, too. He went to sleep on a Saturday night and never woke up. It is the kind of news that hits like the sound of a gunshot at dawn, sending shock down every nerve. He was so alive to every new discovery that death is an incongruity, a misplayed chord, a landscape just glimpsed through a window before the glass shatters.

Coming home this afternoon, I came down the walk just as the afternoon sun burst out from behind a black cloud and poured light into my pear tree. Filled with blossoms at their peak, the tree seemed to flame up like a torch.

I almost hurried past, into the house and the several things I had yet to do before I could relax.

Then, I stopped, put down the bags I was carrying, and just watched glory unfolding around me, as indeed it does every day, every blessed moment. I know that, somewhere inside me. It is only now and then I am reminded how fleeting our chances to see it are.

The Garden was Polly

A garden requires patient labor and attention. Plants do not grow merely to satisfy ambitions or to fulfill good intentions. They thrive because someone expended effort on them. **Liberty Hyde Bailey**

The belly of the country lay swathed in a cummerbund of white clouds. Later, as far as the horizon and haze would allow, the broken chocolate western landscape stretched away.

Still later, as the 737 passed between Needles and Barstow heading for LAX, the landscape became crusted with housing developments, apartment complexes, condominiums, a blistering of mostly red roofs, and jeweled with aquamarine backyard pools, filling the valleys and splashing up on the flanks of the barren hills, the whole mass strung together by progressively thicker strings of roadway, like fungus breeding on the craggy surface of a spoiled orange.

People. As far as I could see, north and south. More than 20 million, I am told, in the Greater Los Angeles area alone.

I had come to say good-bye to one of them, Sue's mother and a friend of mine for only a few years, who had cut a swatch of a time she had loved and held it close.

Polly was a gardener, a keeper of about a half acre and a half century behind her house on a hillside tucked at the feet of the San Gabriels. From one side of the house, on a smogless day, one could see the towers of Los Angeles looming 15 miles away.

Not that there were many smog-free days down there.

She was nearly 90 when she died suddenly at her home. I flew out for the memorial. The family, for the most part, sat around the house; reminisced, pulling their childhoods back up out of the deep cool wells of memory.

I, however, went into the garden. The garden, in a sense, really *was* Polly. She had moved there nearly 60 years earlier, when the house had been one of a few carved out of groves of avocado and orange trees in what was mostly farm country.

Polly

Over the years, the city crept closer, faster every season, and the neighborhood filled with the huge and splashy residences of the rich, the influential, and the just plain showy. The velvety fabric of the nights frayed more often over the years with the sounds of sirens, with the thwap, thwap, thwap of rescue choppers heading into the San Gabriel Mountains to look for the bodies of bikers or motorists who tried a curve too fast on the Angeles Crest highway.

Somehow, Time worked differently in Polly's little half-acre. The orange trees fattened, the avocado tree in the garden grew big as an oak; time there seemed to pause, perch on a stool, scratch its belly, take time, literally, to smell the roses.

But not just roses. There were numerous hybrids of daffodil, amaryllis, "magic" lilies, camellias, iris, clivia, galaxies of flowers that look like daisies trying to become dandelions, forming constellations in all the sunny open spaces. On one arbor grew a tangle of yellow angel trumpet vine, and on another, a riot of bougainvillea. In the right season, the arbor is a tunnel through a cloud of purple so bright it almost hurts the eyes.

Polly Anderson spent her life hybridizing flowers, creating new varieties. There is even a daffodil named after her. For all her tiny stature and soft voice, she bent nature, if only a little, and for a little while, to her considerable will.

I have a photograph of her, standing in a crescendo of lilies, looking old as Aesop, dressed all in red, like the world's first rose.

This trip, I must have taken two dozen photos of the garden, hopelessly. Photographs trap only light. What about the wall of eucalyptus trees sighing in the wind, or the wind whispering through the deodar cedar, its needles moving like smoke? What about the intoxicating essence of a million orange blossoms, or the musky utterance from a thunderhead of wisteria?

Sue and I walked in the garden for a while, shortly before I left to return home. I took many photos for mementos.

I shot the espalier and greenhouse Sue's dad, Ken, had built decades ago, the arbors, and the various angles that gave this little patch of tranquility its peculiar magic.

Then, in the back, where the leaves of a variety of daffodil had fallen over, Sue knelt to check the segment of plastic venetian blind Polly used to identify her newly hybridized flowers. She wrote on them with magic marker.

Sue began weeping hopelessly. She held out the slip of pinkish plastic. Blank. Sun, rain, and time had erased the name. A quick check revealed that this was true of many of the labels.

"This is a whole lifetime of work out here," she said through tears. "And now I can't ask her what anything is."

I can take all the photos I want, but the truth is most of the wonder of the garden will be lost. Film cannot capture the feel of the April breezes, nor the intoxicating glory of the blossoms, the fruity allure of the orange, the musky sweetness of the wisteria.

I brought back a container of soil from her garden to spread in mine. I do not believe in magic, though if I grow anything half so stunning it will surely be a miracle. My motive was sentiment, not alchemy.

I took the red-eye home, hurtling toward morning over cities glittering with cold light, like that emitted by certain deep-sea fishes. What can be said, I thought, about someone ordinary and yet not, as few people are ordinary, after all? She did not invent the transistor or cure cancer; she found no land previously uncharted. How many of us, after all, will be remembered in a century?

The answer, to a near-mathematical certainty, is none. There will be no grim granite obelisk for

Polly, no pigeon-grimed bronze statue of a gnarled old lady carrying a hoe and dibble like a mace and scepter. The little swatch where time faltered will shimmer, recalibrate, and get back in step. The house will be sold. The bulbs in the garden will be lifted lovingly from the refined soil and divvied up between her daughters.

And that will be it. The memories will go on, softened into pale pastel sketches by time, the sharp edges dimmed. There will be grandchildren who remember, fuzzily, a green magic place, blazing with color. These are not bad things. As monuments go, nobody could ask for better.

MAY

Of Cabbage, Peas, and Liniments

It is the time of year when one's enjoyment of gardening is more philosophical than actual.

Everything hurts. If you are a gardener, you know what I mean. Aches, stiffness in the back, suspicious popping sounds in the knees. Sensations heightened by winter inactivity and amplified by the number of springs one already has under one's belt.

I have only had a patch of ground to call my own for a little less than 20 years, so this is all still a voyage of discovery for me.

For example, I have learned that moderation is important. I once used Truck to bring several loads of fresh cow manure to the garden, all of it loaded and unloaded with a shovel.

When I first started working in my little plot, the soil gave the definite impression that it really wanted to be something else. A brick, maybe. When it rained, however, it turned to something the consistency of spackle.

So, enter the manure. A LOT of manure. In my case, it was a layer about two feet thick. Solid.

It was so thick that the tiller mired down to the skid plate in it that spring. Not pretty.

Another time I brought in a mountain of sheep manure. For some reason, sheep manure attracts flies like nobody's business, even in relation to manure from cows and horses. It brought clouds of flies to the neighborhood. Clouds.

Sheep manure may be great for plants, but it does not grow good relations with neighbors, trust me.

In addition to manure, I add vegetable matter, like mushroom soil, composted sawdust or, one year, apple pomace, which is the mealy looking stuff left over after they make apple cider.

Then I grab the rotary tiller and mix the whole mess in with the soil. By the time I plant my warm weather crops, probably late May, everything has begun to break down pretty well.

I, however, start to break down long before the manure does. Keep in mind that I spend most of the year sitting in front of a computer, writing and promising myself to get some exercise. I get more writing done than exercising.

On the plus side, I am in great shape from the wrists to the tips of my fingers.

I was so sore last night, I could hardly struggle up out of my recliner. When it came time to go to bed, I could not get out of the doggone thing.

This is not a good sign, since the garden is only about halfway done. I may be immobile by the time I get the corn in.

On the plus side, I have my peas in, as well as cabbage, two kinds of lettuce, Brussels sprouts, broccoli, arugula, mesclun, onions, and kohlrabi. The latter looks sort of like a turnip, only it is green and grows above ground. It looks like a little alien. I never know whether to eat it or talk to it. Sometimes I do both.

On the negative side, the garden smells like manure and fermenting apples. I smell like manure, fermenting apples, sweat and liniment, and I hurt in places I had forgotten I had.

That is OK, though. Spring is the time of renewal, and I think renewal would not mean as much if it did not take some pain and labor to get there. Besides, beyond the aching joints and sore muscles, I can dream of summer days, surveying my miraculous rectangles of happily thriving vegetables.

I have also learned moderation in what to plant. There really IS such a thing as too many tomato vines. I once planted a dozen or more zucchini plants, thinking that would surely be enough.

I was right.

People still avoid me in summer, fearful that I will be giving away zucchini again. At least, I assume it is the memory of my zucchini giveaway program, and not the memory of the manure

Photo of the top-secret Bovine Manure Cannon. Excellent for gardeners who do not own a pickup truck. Range is classified.

Composure among the Compost

Sometimes I think I am not spiritually fit for gardening.

I have no patience, an ingredient as necessary to gardening as water and fertilizer.

I took up jogging at one time. I got all the way around the track once and I was still fat, so I quit.

I probably watched too many of those science programs when I was a kid. You know, those stop-motion films where the bean seed hops around on the screen like some demented beetle, roots poking and squirming everywhere like so many legs and antennae.

Somewhere in the back of my mind, I think I expect the things I plant to act like that.

Do not get me wrong. I love gardening. I spend time in the bony depths of winter sighing over the pictures in the seed catalogues. When spring is still weeks away, I will find myself poking around in the compost bins, or checking out the clutter of garden tools in the shed, as though some important aspect of them might have magically changed in the months since I placed them there.

In short, I fret.

I got the garden tilled in and half planted. It took most of the weekend. I would have gotten more tilling done, but I managed to break the pull-cord that starts the tiller, which pretty much halted that part of the operation.

Despite the disaster with the machinery, everything was planted that day that was supposed to.

The snow peas are all lined up underneath the poles that will support the vines and fruit. Behind them, in a row of low mounds, the seeds of cantaloupe and watermelon lie snuggled up against cured manure and leaf compost. Nearby, hordes of zucchinis-to-be lurk in similar hills, next to rows of onions, pole beans, and some old tires planted with potatoes.

Behind the garage, on the other side of the snow peas, tomatoes, bell peppers, and jalapeños hide under plastic milk jugs to protect them from the still-chilly nights.

If the weather is decent this weekend, another four rows of corn will appear next to the four I planted last week, along with carrots, spinach, and lima beans.

When I finished last Sunday evening, I sat down, dirty and tired, and surveyed my work. The rows could have been straighter, but overall it did not look bad.

I kept sitting there, on top of a pile of topsoil. Watching.

Waiting.

Idly, I laid about with the trowel, committing murder among the volunteer weeds on the dirt pile.

Then, I meticulously picked up all the clods of dirt within easy reach and ground them up in my hands.

Useful work.

I kept waiting, my mind wandering into all sorts of things, as minds will.

It was getting late.

I checked, for about the third time, the structure I had built for the pole beans to climb. Solid.

Humming some song I could not get out of my mind, I checked the jugs protecting the baby pepper plants. Everything snug.

I put the tools away and locked the shed, and went back to the pile of dirt.

My neighbor came out, on the way to some social engagement.

"Whatcha doin', waiting for somethin' to come up?" he asked, jokingly.

Ha. Ha.

He drove away, and I sat there, feeling silly, because that was exactly what I had been doing.

As I write this, it is just before 7 a.m. The world is wrapped in fog, as something fragile packed for shipping. I just checked the garden for the millionth time this week.

A single, solitary snow pea sprout has shouldered its way past a clod. That is it. One crummy sprout.

"Come on, guys, let's get with it," I said to the assembled and apparently comatose seeds.

It is going to be a long spring.

Draining Ararat

Rain for the past several days, more rain forecast through the near future. I might as well throw out the vegetable seeds and plant rice. Or kelp.

An area behind the raised beds that holds a big pile of manure had become a small lake.

It took some time, but I dug a trench that went across the entire garden to one end of the beds and turned downhill.

All that time, it never stopped raining.

After the ditch was open, I stood there, leaning on the hoe and watching dark stained water drain out of the manure pile into my new ditch. I did not move, partly because I was too tired and partly because my feet were stuck in the mud.

The rain dripped out of my hair and down my neck, but could not seem to cool my head, which burned like a house afire. `I felt gutted, something dark draining slowly out of me and into that sodden and desolate garden.

The problem with depression is that after a while it feels like home, known ground, a familiar tune one can hum without working the memory too hard. As the book title from the 60s, says, "Been Down So Long It Looks Like Up to Me."

Like I said, familiar territory. It runs in the family, an inherited anchor in the cold muck.

I find my own footprints here, faded, the sharp edges blurred. They are all over, as are shreds of me, like tattered clothing caught on fence wire.

Memories, many of which I work very hard not to look at too closely, dot the landscape like junked cars in the front yards of Appalachia.

Yes, perhaps that is where I really live, an Appalachia of the heart. Sounds like the title for a collection of bad poems.

The light grows dim, and the air smells, mysteriously, like burnt feathers.

The heart, we have said, is a house of many rooms. What I have not often said is that so many of the rooms are boarded up, sealed, sometimes to keep things in, sometimes to keep me out. The house, or the livable space in it, is shrinking, I think. I do not know. The dark corners call to me more loudly. I tell myself not to listen. Slyly, I do.

The sun is nearly set, or would be if I could see it though the sullen skies. I am going to walk back out into the garden, though God knows I have spent enough time out there this weekend. I think I am anxious to demonstrate to myself that I can, if not create life, nor create much of anything, at least I can organize something.

Finally, I slog through the garden-shaped pudding, toward the house, where I peel out of my soaked clothes and go inside for a hot shower, and supper.

The next day is sunny, the first in a while. I pull on the rubber boots again and make my way to the garden. It has re-emerged, like a land mass after the biblical flood. In a day or so, the soil will be workable again.

The Ararat-sized pile of manure is high and dry, well, high, anyway, and accessible without SCUBA gear. Standing there with my hands jammed in my pockets, I realize I am grinning.

I have saved the manure.

The crowd goes wild.

Oh, well, not exactly what I was looking for by way of salvation, but I will take it. One takes one's victories as one can find them.

BARKA (Noah's Ark), Dorin Coltofeanu, 2011

Lanterns along the Creek

It could have been a scene from any time in human history.

A group of figures, some young, some not, gathered on the bank of the creek, fishing, talking quietly.

From here, I could not make out any words, only the deep murmur of the men, the lighter tones of the women and children. As dusk deepened, one of them lit a lantern. In a little while, they floated in an island of light in the dark woods and fields across the creek.

I was busy. When I finally went to stand on my deck again, it was 10 p.m. and they were getting ready to leave.

It is funny how much more vast the darkness seems when there is a light in the middle of it. After all, how impressed would we be by the cosmos if there were not any stars scattered like garden-path lights, to show us how very vast it is?

Some ancient peoples used to think that the night sky was a big black dome, filled with pinpricks, or with the stars merely painted on.

In our own European tradition, we figured there were stars and whatnot out there, but we believed that everything rotated around Earth, the entire flickering sweep of creation dancing in homage to humankind.

Later, somebody took a more careful look and figured out it just was not so. They were kicked around pretty good by the church. Nobody likes finding out he is not the center of the universe, even if it is true. Especially if it is true.

The same thing happened when Darwin came along and suggested that all life on earth was related, and that we were not made in the image of God, at least not in the sense that had been thought.

That really got some folks' teakettles steaming. A lot of them are still trying to weasel their way out of that one.

Freud came along a few decades later and cast the first tentative beams of sunlight into the inner workings of the human mind. Not everything he found was pleasant.

In the space of a few hundred years we have gone from being the pinnacle of creation to thinking that we are on our own out here, in a nondescript suburb of a run-of-the-mill galaxy, wheeling around in the dark.

I looked up at my own patch of sky, a ragged tear in the tree line. Small blue pinpricks wheel, spinning their own track farther and farther apart from me and from each other, moment by moment.

The anglers packed up their gear with a clatter of tackle boxes. One of the older ones picked up the gas lantern. Another picked up one of the children, and the little group tottered off, helping one another over obstacles, an irregular dancing of light in the tangled dark.

I thought, as I stepped back into the house to escape the evening chill that was as nice a metaphor for the human story, as I am ever likely to find.

Vegetable Envy

\#   This is the best time of year in the garden, I think. Everything seems possible. The dirt is clean and fresh, beds tidy, seeds tucked in and beginning their magic. I try not to think of Richard Ezell's "50 weeks of anticipation and two weeks of bitter disappointment."

Ahead will be weeds, pests, drought, blights, and hungry deer. But right now, the garden feels like I did when I got out of high school. Look out world.

On the other hand, things get in the way. There is grass to mow, pruning to do, the irrigation pump to tinker with and prime.

Oh, and work. I mean the stuff I do for a living.

I enjoy most of it all, but not all of it equally, and not always when I am actually doing it.

Some days I would like to just sit in the garden and pretend I was one of the vegetables.

Tiller Death Do Us Part

What a day! Went to till the garden, but the trusty 30-year-old Troy-Bilt tiller had some problems. It is a self-propelled rear-tine tiller with big tires, smooth as a Cadillac. I decided that the repairs were just a shade beyond my skill level, and I had plants to get in, so I wrestled it into Truck and ran it out to the local rental center to put it in for repair. They had one remaining rental tiller available, so I went home with a front-tine Honda tiller for the afternoon.

There are debates among gardeners over which are better, front- or rear-tine tillers. After this, I vote hands down for the latter, on humanitarian grounds.

I unloaded the Honda and set-to. It was like holding a wildcat by the rear legs. With our tiller, the propulsion is provided by the big, aggressive tires, which also tend to hold the machine back when the tines are tearing at the ground.

The propulsion in the front-tine machine is provided by the tines digging into the ground. I had to lean backwards to keep it digging, rather than dragging my ass through the neighborhood at 30 mph, screaming like a girl.

That damned thing beat me as if I was a redheaded stepchild.

It only took about an hour to get the tilling done. I cleaned it up, refilled its tank, and returned it.

"Did it perform OK for you?" the friendly fellow at the rental place asked. My hands still throbbed. My shoulders sulked.

"Oh, just fine," I said, which was true enough. It did a lovely job on the soil.

I, however, may not be able to raise my arms above eye level for another week.

Blue Jay Sky and Dancing Carp

The day has sparkled, cool and sunny under a sky the color of blue jays.

Spring so far has seemed more like early autumn, clear, dry air, cool temperatures, and breezy. The garden has greeted all this with suspicion, going on a general strike until only a day or so ago.

The day after temperatures soared into the upper 80s, if only for that day, the garden had sent out emissaries - some black-eyed peas, a few stalks of corn, and some sprouts from my potato patch - apparently as a sort of vote of confidence that summer conditions would soon prevail and they could set about the business of growing in earnest.

A fine spring madness has beset every living thing around here. The yard cats and even our more reserved house cats have been seen batting clods of dirt around in the garden, swatting wind-swayed dandelions, and vaulting high into the air for no apparent reason.

Afterward, when they settle down, it is with a look that seems at once exhilarated and baffled, as though they do not know quite what to make of themselves.

The carp in the creek are still flying off into bouts of giddiness. Celebratory carp. Ardent carp, carp playful as puppies, rolling around on the surface, carp darting back and forth like cats after a ball of yarn.

Carp are such serious, even morose fish. They are, believe it or not, the largest of the minnow family, and native to Asia. They can get to be up to three feet long and weigh 30 pounds. The ones in the creek look to be about the size of Airstream trailers.

Trout one can imagine cavorting, even bass, sunnies, blue gills, but never carp. In the creek on a day when the water is clear, the carp normally seem to chaperone the more frolicsome fish, looming in their schools like flotillas of armored Puritans.

Droopy of countenance, bland of expression, they bring to my mind those broad-beamed and blue-haired dowagers who sailed through the church picnics of my youth like galleons in a harbor full of pleasure craft, censorious and chilling, leaving gloom, if only briefly, in their wake.

Not these carp, nosiree Bob. These carp were everywhere, sucker mouths pumping back and forth in apparent excitement, looking as though they were hooting in astonishment at their own rapture. Imagine, if you can, that a roomful of Puritan elders had suddenly and not entirely of their own will leaped into a frantic dance.

The elders, of course, would have blamed the devil.

I am not sure whom the carp would blame. They were everywhere, appearing up and down that part of the creek.

Here, they sloshed and dithered at the surface, fins stuck out erect, as a child splays his fingers when agitated.

There, along the concrete wall, one carp the size of my upper leg seemed to do a headstand, huge tail flailing the air.

At my feet, a tangled mass of half a dozen carp torpedoed past me, twining about one another like eels.

I stood abashed, even a little embarrassed. Was I witnessing some weird carp mating ritual, a once-a-year orgy in which every carp on the planet simultaneously plays "go fish" in a reproductive frenzy? Is the creek poisoned, and they, in mute pantomime of terror, attempting to flee? Or, are carp simply really very controlled party animals who really, 'way down deep, simply want to boogie?

That is what it was, of course. Our local state game guy told me the carp really lose it when it comes time for, well, you know. They lose all sense and do darned near anything, he said. Being a guy, I have certain sympathy, since it is well known that men have no sense at all when it comes to that sort of thing. Certainly explains many of the predicaments I have found myself in, when all the galumphing and tearing around were over.

I trudged back up the hill to the waiting computer and notes not yet assembled into a story. Behind me, atop the tallest tree across the creek, an orange flame of bird, an oriole, I think, chirruped and sang over a ballroom of dancing fish.

Wrestling with the Rock

When I bought this place nearly 20 years ago, I found it a very strange thing, this idea that I could own a small rectangle of the planet along a small creek near the Mason-Dixon Line.

All these years later, it is still a wonder.

The thing I find strange about owning property is the thing itself, the concept. This occurred to me early in my residency here as I burrowed into the dirt bank under the house. I had been whacking away with a pick around a large and adamant chunk of shale to make some more usable space. Frankly, I was becoming a little fed up with it. Taking the larger of my two crowbars, I jammed and wriggled for a while, until a big piece of it came loose unexpectedly.

There I was, lying on my back, a great, gray-blue stone perched on my stomach.

I swear it snarled at me. Obviously not a Pet Rock-type rock, but one of its feral cousins, not to be trusted in the home, or around small children.

Sprawled there in a staring contest with this chunk of stone (the secret is to not blink,) I could not help but feeling a little bit betrayed. After all, it was my rock.

It had come out of the ground under my house, where it had rested for many millions of years. Dinosaurs had perhaps stubbed their cold-blooded tootsies on this rock. General Abner Doubleday's troops may have complained about its hardness as they slept here during the Battle of Gettysburg.

120

This stone, by golly, has a history, for all its bad attitude.

That is when it hit me. A century from now, when I am reduced to a boxful of rattly bones, this same rock will be sitting wherever I leave it, chortling quietly to itself.

Suddenly, I hated that rock.

What really struck me as funny was the idea that it was mine. Land ownership in this country is largely done in "fee simple," that is, "An estate in land of which the inheritor has unqualified ownership and power of disposition," according to The American Heritage Dictionary.

An odd state of affairs, though understandable. In Europe, from which many of our ancestors came, ownership of land was a more uncertain thing. For that matter, who among those early immigrants would have ever thought, stepping ashore on this vast continent, that deciding how best to use all this land could ever become an issue?

Even today, in some countries, such as Norway, developing productive land is forbidden.

However, land use has become an issue. We have built cities and malls on some the best farmland, a fact that may come back to haunt us. We have poisoned much of the land, and the water within it. We have scattered development all over the green hills. We do this, all unmindful of the costs of providing services to those developments, all for the sake of a pretty view. Too often, the pretty view becomes yet another development.

Naturally, I have no answers to this dilemma, only questions. I would not champion the surrender of control over my little piece of ground. Yet I would cry loud and long if my neighbor yielded to a deep and so-far secret desire to raise, say, hogs in the space between our houses.

A prediction: The more crowded we become, the more we will find ourselves qualifying our degree of ownership, the more "power of disposition" we will surrender, perhaps not always willingly.

I say this with neither glee nor despair but in a kind of resignation, to the realities of this place, where people not very different from me came desiring Eden but stayed to live, clumped into ticky-tacky neighborhoods coyly named and depressingly like their clone neighborhoods everywhere else.

Now, if I can just get this rock of my chest, I can get back to work.

JUNE

<u>Epiphany at Tillietown</u>

The storm came out of the south and west, brawling down off the eastern slopes of the Blue Ridge to kick through the forests and fields, make sheets flutter like torn sails, and harass the tin of barn roofs.

It came after several days of misty rain, with temperatures neither hot nor cold and the air too sticky with moisture to be comfortable. The air boiled, giddy with tossed leaves and flung birds. The ground shook.

I stepped out of a downtown restaurant to discover that the western sky had turned to scorched pewter.

I had an errand to run, but it would wait. I jumped in my pickup and took off down the Lincoln Highway, chasing that sunset.

When I was a little boy, I always thought that if I looked closely enough at the ragged sunset edges of storms I would see heaven. I figured whole squadrons of angels were out there, arrayed around the edges of the fiery clouds, admiring the tumult below and generally keeping an eye on things.

In my imagination, it looked very much like scenes from the copies of classical paintings that graced our big family Bible. I thought that if I could get in an airplane, I could ride through that hole in the storm and get to heaven without having to die.

I am older now, and a little more jaundiced about the idea that there are angels looking out for us, and about my ability to get into heaven under any circumstances, except possibly by an error in the celestial paperwork.

Still, I am drawn to storms, as I have said, especially to their borders, where chaos meets calm.

I chased the storm's edge for some time, and finally had to stop and get out of the truck, if only in the interest of public safety. I was not doing so well at watching the road.

I was just down the road from a place where I once lived, where I used to watch the storms come marauding off South Mountain to ruffle the apple orchard at the old Deardorff farm before slamming into the wall of the house.

My first thought as I stopped the truck was to wish I would have brought my camera. Then I thought better of it. You have all seen postcards of sunsets, and you all know how cheesy they look compared to the real thing.

Just try to imagine a sky aflame with color: peach, silver, white, and a deep purple fading to black, all cut to tatters in the wind and swirling like confetti. Picture it all sailing majestically over the dark mass of the western mountains, as banks of mist rise in the valley, in some places nearly as high as the clouds themselves. Think of swifts darting and swirling over the fields, whether merely chasing bugs or playing with the wind, I do not know.

Just in front of me, flotillas of geese patrolled in silhouette in a pond that mirrored the sky. An artist friend once said that only God could create such a scene without it looking tacky. She was right.

A flash made me turn to the east. Within the arc of a rainbow, lightning laced the blackness where the storm still thrashed. It was almost too much - the clouds and mists, the pond, rainbow, and now a filigree of lightning. I believe that if the sky had opened up to reveal comets dancing a tarantella, I would not have been surprised.

I do not know how long I stood there in the spitting rain, trying to take it all in. Eventually, though, the glory in the west began to fade, and the rainbow dissolved like sugar in water. I climbed slowly back into the truck and started home.

Still on one of the back roads, I passed a little house in the middle of a large, square lot. From the front porch they would have had a front row seat to the show. There were cars parked outside and lights on, everybody safely tucked inside. I could see the glow of a television screen. I wanted to go bang on the door, drag them outside to see what I would just seen, but thought better of it. Everybody has to find his own view of heaven. I got back to my errand, and then went home.

Pinhole

"If the doors of perception were cleansed, every thing would appear to man as it is, infinite. For man has closed himself up, till he sees all things thro' narrow chinks of his cavern." **William Blake**

Remember that old saying, "What you see is what you get?"

Forget about it.

There is a lot more out there that you will never see, hear, or smell.

It has been a little more than 30 years since I found out about all this and I am still p.o.'d.

Imagine stuffing cotton balls in both ears and up your nostrils, then pulling a pasteboard box over your head with a single wee pinhole poked in it for you to see through, and you' have an idea about how we make our way through the world.

It is a wonder more of us do not break our necks.

What you see, hear, and smell is just a sample of what is out there. The human eye and its wiring see only a very narrow range of the radiation (that is what you see, you know, energy...) that's flying around out there. Bees, moths, and other critters can see a lot further onto either side of the visual spectrum.

The same goes for our hearing. We are practically deaf, compared to many of our neighbors on the planet. Watch your dog sometime, tilting his head this way and that into the shadows at night, apparently growling at nothing.

Or watch him sampling the breeze of a summer evening. Heck, he is reading the Encyclopedia Britannica while you are over there cleaning out your ears with your car keys and reading the church bulletin.

When I finally put together all this stuff I had learned, I caught myself standing stock-still in a public garden somewhere, looking around and wondering what I was missing.

To quote some famous figure in baseball, "We was robbed!"

There are a number of so-called primitive societies that believe this whole experience we call the "real world" is nothing but a dream or an illusion.

We have always looked down on people like that and called them ignorant. I am not so sure anymore.

SUMMER

*Gardens are not made by singing 'Oh, how
beautiful,' and sitting in the shade.* **R.Kipling**

Hot Solstice

Just outside my office window, slightly more than
half way across the creek, sits a stone we have
taken to calling turtle rock, for the simple reason
that we have seen upwards of six turtles of about
the size of salad plates sunning themselves on it.

This morning turtle rock stood high above the
algae-littered surface. By afternoon, though we had
no rain here, thunderstorms in the western hills
had shrunk the little island to half its size, and by
dusk, it was under water completely.

This time of year the creek is as variable as the
weather, now slatey and opaque, a moment later
glittering in the sun. Its level, too, changes, up and
down, like a great serpent breathing.

The day I write this is the summer solstice, when
the sun at noon hangs directly over the Tropic of
Cancer and night and day fall in equal length on
either side. Now we begin the long slide toward
autumn and each day will be a little shorter,
though the days will become hotter, as the
accumulated heat in the ground and the patterns
of wind keep summer on us with the tenacity of a
snapping turtle.

The garden charges ahead full bore. The creek is
full, but heading for the low levels of the summer
drought. It is summer, high gear and warp drive
for the creek and garden both.

Fireflies

In the winter, I forget about fireflies.

I do not know how this happens. How can I be so jaded to take them for granted? I guess it is because there are so many of them we think of them as common, simply so much background glitter.

Late one evening I stood in the driveway taking in the night. The fields stuttered with a galaxy of fireflies, blinking the lusty Morse code of their brief mating season.

The black expanse under the clouded sky swarmed with them, as though the Milky Way had come down after all this time to see what all the commotion was.

Taking fireflies for granted makes sense, I guess. As we grow up, we like to act cool, as if we know it all.

Miraculous old world. Ho-hum.

The firefly is doubly misnamed, in fact.

The light has nothing to do with fire. The firefly's scientific name, Lampyridae, means "torchbearers." In addition, it is not a fly, but a beetle.

America has about 100 species of firefly out of 2,000 across the globe. Each has its own flash pattern.

The members of a Southeast Asia species flicker their taillights in unison. Must be quite a sight.

The light show you see in the open on summer evenings are the males of the species, looking for a little girlie action.

The females remain on the ground, mostly out of sight, flashing back.

One naturalist wrote that the males can be attracted by squatting near the ground and flashing a penlight at two-second intervals. I have never tried it, so I do not know if it works.

The fireflies' light, called "bioluminescence," is caused by the internal mixing of two substances in the bug's body called, wonderfully, "luciferin" and "luciferase." Do not be alarmed. The materials were not named after the devilish Lucifer, but after the one in Greek myth, the light-bearer who brings in the dawn.

Almost all of the chemical energy expended by the firefly results in light.

Compare that to the light of a 100-watt incandescent bulb; 94 percent of the energy it takes to run it is wasted producing heat.

JULY

The Devil in Barlow

"The most beautiful thing we can experience is the mysterious. It is the source of all true art and all science. He to whom this emotion is a stranger, who can no longer pause to wonder and stand rapt in awe, is as good as dead: his eyes are closed."

A. Einstein, 1931

If I had been paying more attention to my driving, I would have missed it.

A dust devil, a big one, kicking up a fuss in a freshly harvested field.

When I was a kid, I used think they were baby tornadoes. A favorite game was to run into them, to see what they would do. The really little ones would break up, as though I had killed them. Maybe I had. Now and then, one would be big enough to get me off balance and I would fall. Fair enough, I suppose.

As I got a little older, I played with the idea that they might be, after all, some sort of supernatural entity. One could almost believe it, seeing one darting around the pitcher's mound on the playground at school, a funnel of dust 50 feet high, tossing leaves and paper scraps high in the air.

Science tells us they are only spirally rotating high velocity winds that rarely last more than 15 minutes and hardly ever rotate faster than 50 mph. They occur during times when the ground heats up quickly with a cooler air mass lying over it. The dust is incidental, and one can travel over a debris-free area and be essentially invisible. Call them stealth devils.

Science also tells us there is evidence of dust devils on Mars, and on Triton, one of the moons of Neptune. The ones on Triton may be more than six miles in height, with tails extending horizontally for more than 60 miles.

I saw this local one just after I had made a left turn onto the Barlow Road, between two fields. It danced along, throwing dust, small clods of dirt, and dried corn leaves all over the place, traveling the length of the field at a pace a little slower than I was driving. I pulled onto the shoulder, stopped the engine, and walked to the side of the field to watch.

The devil slowed and stopped, about 100 feet away, dancing back and forth over a small area. I could hear the rustle of the leaves, and the small sound of dirt clods bumping along the rough ground. I looked at my watch. I was not going to make the staff meeting. The devil wiggled a little, teasing me. I dare you, it seemed to say.

I checked my watch again. The devil tossed a piece of white paper, a page from a newspaper, I think, high in the sky. I climbed back into my van and drove away. The devil swayed in the middle of the field, wearing a crown of dust and leaves.

The staff meeting started late, so I was on time. Would have been on time, in fact, even if I had yielded to temptation and run through the devil, to see if I could knock him down.

After the meeting, the editor asked me if there was anything new in my neck of the woods.

I almost told him there was a devil dancing in a field in Barlow, but thought better of it.

Dust Devil

Drought

Lately, I have observed that watching the creek in drought is like watching a dragon sleep.

The water, murkier now than usual, is a kind of greenish brown, jeweled with sky colors when teased by the wind, black and mysterious in twilight, reflecting more than it reveals.

Sometimes when it is sunny and dry here, it will rain in the hills, where the creek arises. This makes the stream here swell slowly, and then

Marsh Creek in August

recede, as though the dragon is breathing.

Despite the long dry spell, the creek is a lively place. In the early mornings, if I am lucky, I can see both green and blue herons feeding in the shoals.

134

Lately, a pair of ospreys has been raising a ruckus in the woods on the far bank, their clear cries echoing all day. I think they have nested, but I have not been able to spot it. I have no idea why they make so much noise.

The carp have been mostly invisible, except for the clouds of silt they raise as they feed. If I stand very still for a while, the two beavers whose burrow lies almost directly opposite my office window will come out to feed.

Canada geese feed almost every late afternoon on underwater vegetation in the shallows, and occasionally take time out for a very noisy social event. They bathe, ducking, so to speak, entirely underwater, then ruffle their feathers. This ritual is always accompanied by little turf battles and a great deal of honking.

Rarely far away is the snapping turtle. I think of him as the Grim Reaper. A big fellow probably 18 inches from the tail to snout, he is the reason there are not more geese here. He takes his tithe from the population of young every year.

He floats, big as a plate, in the middle of the creek, his clawed feet splayed out, his head with its gash of a mouth sticking out of the water just far enough for him to breathe.

He is also, I might add, the main reason I wear shoes when I wade in the creek. I have enough trouble with math without losing digits.

As I write, the creek is higher than it has been in weeks. Yesterday a line of thunderstorms rumbled through the area, rattling the windows as though every Harley in the world had just driven by, all at once.

I stood, shirtless, in the storm for a while, enjoying the cold sting of the rain. After it was all over, the plants in the garden had lost their wilt, and the some of the shoals in the creek were once again submerged.

The rain gauge registered less than half an inch. It was not enough, not by far. It will not set the water table where it should be, or be of much help to crops. But I will take it.

Volkswagens in Love

The flower garden was going pretty well until recently, when I noted that a number of leaves had gone to lace, as though putting on airs.

Japanese beetles.

As a kid, I always thought Japanese beetles were kind of pretty, like small jewels.

That was then. This is now.

Now, there they were, uncountable clusters of them. I swear, on quiet afternoons I can hear them chewing.

So, what to do? I have no experience in these matters. A friend suggested a new kind of trap, the nature of which I still find vaguely disquieting.

Apparently, bug scientists have come up with bait for these traps that not only attracts the beetles, but also fills them with desire. No, not desire; raw, drooling lust is more like it.

"It is really simple," my friend said. "The beetles are fooled into this mating frenzy, and then they fall into this trap and can't get out."

Frankly, it sounded an awful lot like my life during my 20s and 30s. Putting my queasiness aside, I got some of the traps and placed them in strategic positions around my garden.

Oh, my.

It is a scene I find nearly impossible to describe without leaping far beyond the boundaries of good taste. Think of an armored office Christmas party, or an orgy of animated beans. Think of Volkswagens in love.

The idea behind the traps is that there is this little thing that holds the bait, some little sponge or something sopping with lust-making beetle pheromone juice. The beetles, thoroughly porcupined by Cupid's arrows, clamber all over the upper part of the trap and, in this case, the branch to which it is tied, cheerfully greeting and getting to know 20 and 30 of their best friends, one after the other.

Finally, exhausted, they fall into an hourglass-shaped plastic bag, from which there is no escape.

They do not stop, um, greeting one another in the bag either. I made the mistake of picking one of the bags up in my cupped hand when it must have had a couple hundred beetles in it. I will probably have nightmares forever.

Nightmares aside, the traps worked. Sure enough, the cannas, the ones that have not already been turned into brown doilies, are standing in the sunshine un-munched and peaceful.

The question arose of what to do with this embarrassment of beetles once they have greeted themselves into a stupor. I heard that they make great fish bait, so I took a squirming bagful to the back yard and dumped them into Marsh Creek.

A shimmering wad of Japanese beetles plopped into the water and bobbed to the surface, separating as they made it to the surface. A few managed to drag themselves up onto the bank, there perhaps to reflect on what must have seemed a remarkable day.

The remainder of the flotilla paddled around in the grip of the main current, swinging out into the broad body of the creek above the dam. It was still the hot part of the day, so the big fish had not yet started feeding, but a few smaller fish began to thin the numbers of the convoy, some of whom seemed to be merely waving their legs around drunkenly.

Perhaps they still thought they were at the party.

The galaxy of dizzy jewels drifted out of my perception. It would be twilight soon. I did not think they would be swimming for long.

The thought struck me as I headed back up the hill that whatever substance so love-struck the beetles might make its way into the fish population of the creek. By that time the next day, Marsh Creek could be filled to the brim with randy bass, lovesick carp, and catfish inclined to compose bad verse. What have I done? I thought.

I went to the tree to sling the plastic bag back under the bait. The leaves on the branch above bore a darkly shimmering mass of very friendly beetles.

"The wages of sin is death!" I yelled. Nobody listened. Nobody ever does.

Inspiration from Above

The great thing about epiphanies is that you just never know when they are going to happen.

An expected epiphany would be a contradiction in terms.

On a recent Sunday, I stood coffee in hand, looking out over the creek, the trees, and the critters I could see.

I had been watching a great blue heron in the bright sunlight, spearing his breakfast in the rocky shoals. Something caught my eye, a glittering movement, a bright sparkling thread of light, a chain of diamonds trailing from the branch of the big oak right outside the window.

First, you have to understand that I love nature writing. My shelves are crowded with books by Loren Eiseley, David Hopes, Henry Beston, Edwin Way Teale, Annie Dillard, and the like.

Through them, I have learned that as vast as the world may be, there is enough wonder and horror in the average back yard to keep me goose-bumpy and awake many a night.

Eiseley wrote of playing with a fox kit, and of dancing with, I think, a Sand Hill crane. Teale and his wife tracked all four seasons as they made their way across the U.S. Beston wrote stirringly that animals are "different nations" with attributes different and sometimes better than our own. Dillard wrote a passage about the death of a frog in the jaws of a giant water bug that still gives me the willies just thinking about it.

Now, you would think that after so much reading about the finned, feathered, furred, hooting, clacking, chirping world would have prepared me for just about anything.

That was before I saw the squirrel pee.

Yeah, I know, all God's creatures gotta go. It is just not something one thinks about. Gathering nuts for the winter. Running helter-skelter into the paths of cars. Scolding the cats from the tree branches. Building nests of leaves in the branches of trees. Eating the stalks of my corn plants, (Which had me telling the cats that for all the free food they were mooching off me, they could try a little predation once in a while. They just blinked and told me to talk to the shop steward.)

Nobody ever mentioned, well, squirrels' bathroom habits.

There he was, in full sun on a thick branch, letting go, his tail and head held high. He looked like he was smiling, but I may just be projecting. The, um, product ran off the branch and trailed off to the leaf litter far below, making the glittering chain that had caught my eye.

He finished his business, flicked his tail a couple of times, and launched himself into the air to another branch. Back to work, scolding, nut gathering, and so on. It is a tough life.

I stood there, finishing my coffee, happy to be reminded that there is always something new to learn from nature. One just has to pay attention, to be still, and be open to new possibilities. Not a bad lesson on a Sunday morning.

I resolved to spend more time walking along the creek, and in the woods.

And to always wear a hat.

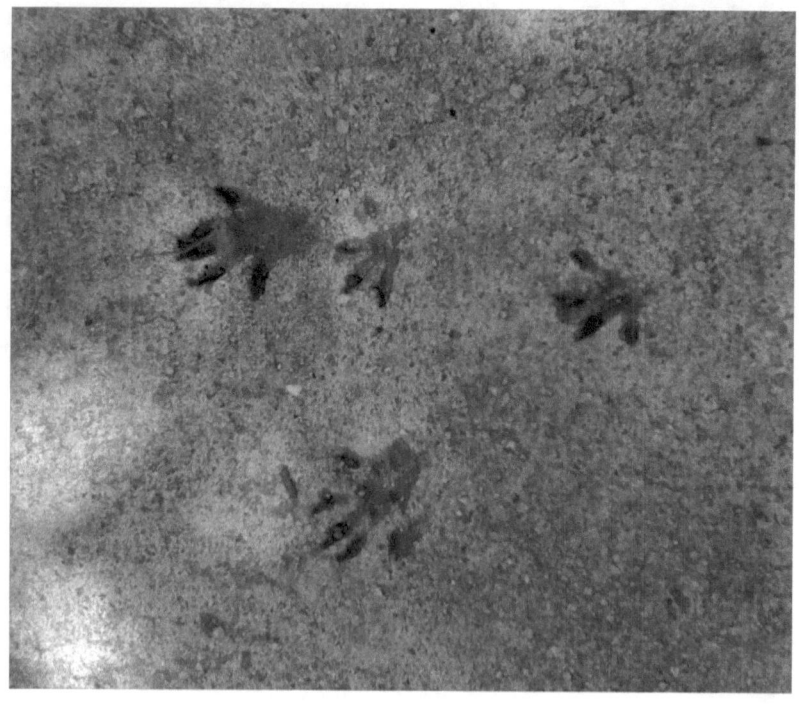

Squirrel tracks

Eagle

It was just dumb luck that I saw it, swooping from a branch on the other side of the creek.

A bald eagle.

It dropped toward the creek, directly toward where I stood doing some chores around the house. The eagle banked sharply to my right, rowed the air for a few seconds, and then glided to a high branch on another tree.

I blinked a few times. Camera, I thought. Where is the camera?

I had seen this eagle, or one like it, several times in the general area since March, but this is the first time in the years I have been living along this creek that they have shown up right here, in my back yard. The birds are rare enough that most folks think they only live in the mountains, along the northeastern coast, or maybe in the Florida swamps.

In fact, the bird's natural range used to run across Alaska and Canada and down through almost all of the lower 48 states.

That was the old days, of course. Between the use of the now-banned insecticide DDT, and yahoos shooting them, by 1963, only 417 eagles were found in the lower 48 states. In 1978, the U.S. Fish and Wildlife Service declared the bald eagle to be an endangered species.

The birds have been doing well enough that the bald eagle was delisted in 2007. As of that year, the U.S. Fish and Wildlife Service counted nearly

10,000 breeding pairs of bald eagles in the 48 contiguous states.

This is not to say they are as common as the Canada geese that are always quarreling in the creek, so I went and got the camera, and slipped quietly to the side of the creek and waited.

It was the flash of white in the tree branches tipped me off. The big raptor stepped into the air as though the atmosphere was its own private limo, and winged upstream. I got the new digital camera up, got the eagle in the viewfinder, and pressed the button.

Nothing happened, except the viewfinder drew little brackets around the figure of the eagle of which I was NOT getting a photo.

Finally, I gave up on the camera, and just watched the eagle beat its way around the bend and out of sight. I forgot to be irritated about the camera and stood there feeling as though I had just received a great gift.

Pet Vultures

I came around a corner of a friend's barn on my way to put out some food for the band of cats that live there when I saw something odd.

Standing patiently around the cats' bowls were three black turkey vultures, an adult and two fledged chicks.

The adult flew away, but the chicks flew only as far as a horizontal beam on the lean-to on the back of the barn and kept a cautious watch. I went in to the stall, brought out the cat food, and filled the bowls.

The chicks fidgeted a bit. I put the cat food away and walked out, very matter-of-fact and stood still, watching. A couple of the cats came up and started to feed. One of the chicks flew away.

The remaining chick stayed behind, watching me. Maybe sizing me up for a future buffet.

"Do not start polishing the silver yet, Bozo," I said. "I feel OK."

The Garden Where the Wild Things Are

Let us turn elsewhere, to the wasps and bees, which unquestionably come first in the laying up of a heritage for their offspring. **Jean Henri Fabre**

It is high summer. The sky looks like hot pewter and the air feels like a wet St. Bernard.

In the untended sections of the garden, the soil lies pale as flour, sending up little mushroom clouds of dust when struck by drops from the water hose. The leaves of the zucchini, butternut and banana squash scarcely stir.

Being a guy, what I tell people is that gardening is better than watching television: No commercials and a lot more sex and violence. For the bugs, anyway.

It is, after all, a savage place, these 1600 square feet or so of tilled earth.

In every section, ladybugs prowl, munching their way through aphids like a teenager eating French fries.

In the dense tangle of tomato vines, caterpillars, fat and doomed, crawl listlessly, their backs decorated with rows of clean white, tapered wasp eggs. Think of it as an early form of take-out.

In the broccoli, the cabbage moth larvae fare as badly. Shiny black wasps come to sting the busy cabbage worms. Paralyzed but still alive, the worms are carried away by the laboring wasp, to be hidden away in some secret den, lying unnaturally still next to the wasp's eggs.

The wasp grubs eat the worms from the inside out. The caterpillar survives, for a little while.

If you let it get to you, a garden is a temple of nightmares.

The high priest is, without question, the implacable praying mantis, a thoroughly Old Testament demon of a bug, lurking and angular, with a triangular head that can turn to watch as you walk past.

The mantis eats anything it can snare in its death-trap front legs, up to and including small rodents.

Not a place to be taken lightly, this garden.

A thunderstorm tore through a few days ago, tousling the garden. The first wash of the storm pushed the tangle of tomatoes to the leeward, worried at the cornrows and caused the black-eyed peas to flail around like sinners at a tent revival.

In the corn, as the sun reappeared, a mantis cleaned itself after a meal, keeping an eye open for new prospects. As the sun broke through over the cabbage, the air buzzed, dark with wasps.

High Water

A freak storm waded through the mid-state recently with wind, lightning, and heavy rain. The area where we live received a foot of rain in five hours. I walked out on the deck on a whim to take a shower in the rain, just so I could say I had. It hurt. The next morning my upper body was bruised and sore. Yes, it was a dumb idea.

In the first 30 minutes of the storm, Marsh Creek rose eight feet.

This afternoon I walked down to the creek-side to retrieve a rock that had rolled downhill from a terrace I am building. I stood for several minutes looking at the scruffy late summer surface of the creek, rippled here and there by feeding fish and turtles.

I realize that I have not even been in the creek yet, and here it is the end of July. Between the job and all the things to do with a "fixer-upper" house, I hardly even take time to sit by the creek and just try to take it in.

It is worth the time when I do. The herons are long since back, pale and gaunt and stalking the shallows. To our delight, the osprey has come back as well, full grown, with a wingspan that must reach three feet or better. Last weekend as I stood talking with a neighbor the osprey flew overhead, silhouetted against the sky, a fish clenched in his talons.

The House the Amoeba Built

A good friend who is always making my mind stretch sent me a photo of an amoeba's house.

Do not be fooled by the photo. The real thing is the size of the period at the end of this sentence.

This kind of stuff tickles me cross-eyed.

This particular variety of amoeba surrounds its little shapeless body with tee-tiny pebbles and squats happily indoors, doing whatever amoebas do when they are not eating bits of organic material by wrapping around them and reproducing by splitting in two. Maybe watching Sponge Bob Squarepants re-runs.

Anyway, the little house has a little scalloped doorway and little projections sort of like fins in the back. It is shaped sort of like a cartoon rocket ship.

This is what Liz said:

"I loved the description of what happens to the second generation – one gets the house and the other gets the pile of building materials that the "parent" saved up to start a new one. It just seemed so humble and simple and fair – and yeah, flabbergasting. It also made me think we probably make too much of our own achievements. We may stack'em higher, but I have never seen anything

cuter or sweeter in a house. Just the right size, safe and cozy, mobile, home-made (I almost said "handmade"), a real masterpiece of folk art by some teeny tiny folk.

No, there's nothing random about it."

The "random" remark came about because we both know that Creationists would point at this little house as somehow "proving" that life is way too complicated to have occurred by chance, which is how they misconstrue evolution.

But evolution is not a crapshoot. It is a perfectly logical – and demonstrable – system of thought. The Creationists might as well argue that the fact that bees wear stripes rather than paisley is proof that god wove the fabric himself.

The little house is a delight, plain and simple, because over billions of years of life on earth, it is just one of those wonderful surprises that evolved along with the rest of us. Every very gasping, wriggling one of us is a freaking miracle, no deity needed, thank you very much.

Slugs and a Brain Full of Stew

The other day brought one of those episodes one gets from thinking too much. While exploring the further reaches of the freezer a package of frozen leftover spareribs came to light. Hoary with freezer burn, I dumped them out along the front walkway for the benefit of the loose affiliation of cats that patrol the neighborhood.

Late the next night, stepping outside to take in the night air, a glistening caught my eye. A network of lazy, glittery lines crossed the concrete path from various points, converging on the jumble of small bones, which itself glowed, reflecting the yard light.

Up close, the explanation was clear: A squadron of very large slugs had assembled on the bones, and was scraping away at whatever nourishment the cats had left behind.

Ribs are ribs, and baby back ribs look not altogether different from people ribs, and I suddenly had a short, sharp image of dozens of slugs crawling around over my own rib cage. I performed a dance of revulsion down the path to the house and locked the door, and actually thought briefly of nailing it shut. Some images are not to be borne.

In the morning, the bones were as clean as old sticks.

I should not have been surprised. My brain does things like that to me when I have been poking around in matters it finds uncomfortable. The villain in this most recent episode was the June issue of National Geographic; in particular, the article by Joel Swerdlow entitled "Quiet Miracles of the Brain."

Articles on brain function are a sort of minor hobby of mine, for the simple reason that the three pounds or so of gray jelly is, as one of the scientists quoted in the Geographic said, the most complex object in the known universe.

The problem with looking into science to any depth is that what you find there too often conflicts with the ways one is used to thinking about one's own universe. Darwin's theories upset so many people because they did not like to think of themselves as evolved from other animals, not because Darwin's science was questionable.

That is as true today as it was back then, when science knew a lot less. I have had people who have never in their lives read a book on biology or genetics tell me in all seriousness that the theory is "ridiculous." Never mind that farmers and pet breeders have been exercising a homegrown version of evolution for all of recorded history.

At any rate, Swerdlow said that scientists argue more and more "everything we experience can be reduced to a physical component."

Candace Pert, a researcher interviewed for the article, took it a little further when she said chemicals called neuropeptides create all emotions. All love, joy, grief and so on for everyone is created by the action of scores of neuropeptides acting on our various mental buttons and switches.

Think about it. Rather puts things like poetry, music, art, a passion for '57 Chevrolets and screaming guitars into a different perspective does it not?

One of my best friends chided me about that statement *"Just kill me, Terry. This shit is magic and you know it, and I refuse to believe otherwise."*

I sympathize, believe me. As a semi-retired poet and artist and a dabbler in the written arts, I do not really know what to do with this information. My first, and I suspect a common, reaction is to cut and run and have nothing to do with it.

But really, is it harder to live with than the idea of, say, Cupid? Who wants one's love life ruled by some chubby airborne brat with a bow and arrow? In my experience, his aim has not always been what it could have been.

Like Darwinism, these assorted discoveries regarding brain chemistry are both disappointing and fascinating, and I am still trying to sort out my feelings about them. On the other hand, maybe my chemicals are bubbling along trying to come to terms with it all, stewing things over, in a sense.

The real problem comes in thinking about that new, hard-scientific reality with an old-fashioned mind trained to believe in things like love, grief, and joy that were emotions and nothing more or even reflections of some divine spark.

That my reactions to anything at all may be the concoction of some mobile mulligan stew is something from which my poor old-fashioned wiring shies away. Maybe I will go read something else, perhaps some poetry, to try to break the spell a little. That, and sprinkle a little salt on the snails. Sorry, guys.

AUGUST

Journal

Somehow, it is August.

The summer creeps at you in May, as you muck about in the garden, wondering if that cold grim dirt you have been freezing your hands in every weekend would ever produce anything.

Then, after the weeding, watering, and feeding, the new miracle of the new season, by August, has suddenly mutated into a tangled disappointment, with too many squash, not enough corn, and a few things that did not bother to show up at all.

That is the trouble with gardens, of course. They never quite turn out the way you had thought they would.

I do not know why I let these things surprise me. One of the first things you learn working in a newsroom is that life is what happens to you while you were making other plans.

Owls

Outside, through the open windows here in the dining area, the owl hoots once, bringing to mind ghost stories, and endless Westerns, where the hoot of an owl nearly always meant the proximity of Indians. The Indians, whom we now call by the leaden title "Native Americans," were, in their film version at any rate, objects of fear, dread and awe. The reason, one suspects, is they were somehow a part of that "out there" behind and within that black wall of trees, the world where birds exist with wings a dozen feet wide.

It was not our world. For most of us now, what passes for Nature is lamp-lit, with traffic hissing on the hard roads under our windows, trees reduced to ornamental shapes in the yard, their rectangular perfection strapping chaotic Nature into the petty geometry of our fear.

It is the secret of gardens and lawns that they are amulets of sorts, a charm against the tangle of the world from which we have arisen and which we cannot leave behind. We hear the owl and our hackles rise, a response left over from when we had fur to bristle; our ears prick, even to the point of moving, using muscles most of us have forgotten we possess and which few of us can control purposefully.

Tree in the Net

I am one of those people who are frequently in the right place at the right time.

I do not understand why this should be. It just is. I once sat on a creek-side stone and had a hawk land on a dead branch not five feet away. We looked at one another for a few moments. Then he stepped off the branch, glided down the bank and over the water.

I felt as though I had been passed an encrypted message, one that I have never been able to decode. Maybe the message itself is the meaning.

These things have happened to me all my life. A friend once asked me how I do it, as though there were some trick. My reply was that one has to go through the world receptive to miracles, but not looking for them. It was not the answer he wanted, but is that not the way it always is.

This morning, I went out about daylight to get the morning paper, and stood for a while to take in the dawn. A heavy fog had arisen during the night, and the entire world lay secret, the way children will hide under a blanket.

So thick lay the fog by the creek that the entire world seemed to consist of this little group of houses, a gravel road that bowed from horizon to horizon, and Marsh Creek, the ocean of this little patch of ground.

I looked up at the tree that stands in my dooryard. The fog clung to spider webs in the outer twigs in front of me. As I looked closer, I saw the entire tree festooned with spider webbing, long strands looping from twig to twig, as though some ethereal fisherman had caught it by accident and torn his

nets.

I have no idea whether that tree has been bound and gagged all spring and summer, or if something strange and wonderful happened to it just the night before. I have walked under those branches hundreds, thousands of times, and never seen the gossamer bindings. Of course, I never before simply stood there and just looked, receptive, ready.

Last night as twilight fell, a thin young man and his son stood fishing on the opposite bank. I loitered at the door outside my office watching as they struggled to attach something, a lure, I suppose, to the boy's line.

So intent were they on the mysteries of tying knots that our local beaver swam by, not 30 feet away, and they never saw it. It crossed my mind to yell and call their attention to it, but thought better of it. It would only annoy the beaver.

After the man and boy left, I walked out again to enjoy the failing light. Just as I stepped out onto the deck, a heron rose up out of the trees at the little cove just out of sight and flew downstream, wing tips teasing the water. He was all grace and symmetry, an elegant shape the color of a river-worn stone.

He passed swiftly into the dusk like a prayer of thanksgiving. I went back into the house, duly blessed.

Random

The woman died at about the same time I noticed the rain.

I sat at the table overlooking the creek, peacefully listening to the combined sounds of birdsong and my teeth crunching away at Cinnamon Puffins cereal. Music played softly on the kitchen radio. Sue worked on a crossword puzzle. I thought about checking my work email, and then thought better of it.

It began to rain on the creek, thousands of circles spreading from each drop, intersecting, and setting off secondary waves. The entire pattern was dependent on each drop. Take one away; add one, and the pattern changes. I suppose a mathematician could calculate where each ring would go, what consequences each intersection would have. On the surface, literally and figuratively, it seemed very random.

The rain only fell on one side of the house, I noted with interest. Obviously, when it rains or snows, there is a line where it ends. If I believed in portents, I would have thought it portended something. A random event with delusions of omen.

Downstream about three-quarters of a mile as the heron flies, and at about that moment, a 12-passenger van filled with three vacationing families heading for Niagara bounced off a guardrail at the bridge over my creek, hit another guardrail, crossed the median and slammed into a third.

One of the passengers, Eun Ju Lee, 36, of Oklahoma City, a young mother of two, was thrown from the van and died as I crunched away at my Puffins upstream.

That same day, 63 years earlier, Sumiko Koide, 17, was carrying her baby sister in the alley between her parents' home and a neighbor's, when the sun came to Earth.

The Koide family lived about 20 minutes by car from downtown Hiroshima.

It was not, of course, a random act in any sense of the word, but to the tens of thousands killed and injured, it probably seemed so, on that tranquil summer morning. It was 8:15 a.m., local time. I can easily imagine people sitting at breakfast, looking out their windows.

Sumiko told me she remembers a silent flash, then chaos.

"I saw so many dead people. So many walking with the skin dropping off of their faces and hands, so many with their faces terribly bloated," she said.

A few days later, the sun came to Earth over Nagasaki.

Another raindrop, another circle spreading, hitting other circles. Thousands upon thousands of random circles removed, altering the paths of those remaining.

Predictable? Maybe. But it still feels random. I asked Sumiko if she thought dropping the two bombs helped to shorten the war, or in the end, saved lives.

"I do not know. I guess there would have been more people die in an invasion. But not all in one place," she said. "It is hard to say that it should have been bombed."

She was quiet for a bit, then added: "We would not have given up, I think, if not for the bombing," adding that each home had bamboo spears beside the front door in the event of an American invasion. Everyone, children included, had strict instructions from the government what to do when the Americans came.

"We were each to kill one and then ourselves. We were not to surrender," she said.

A few months before his death, I interviewed physicist and biologist Ray Crist about the Manhattan Project, which led to the creation of the two bombs. Crist was 105, and had only recently retired from teaching.

"...There was really no morality (about it). There was a real chance of the Germans getting it and we knew they were working on it. It was a question of war. It had gone beyond morality. Everybody was terrified of the Germans finding this first. It was a matter of life and death," he said.

After the war, Crist was one of a group of scientists invited to travel to the Far East and witness a demonstration of an atomic bomb blast. He declined.

"I did not want to go. I did not want to get a personal sense of what the bomb would do," he said.

Indeed. Who would?

On the way home from work last night, I stopped briefly at the scene of the accident. As it happened, I was listening to some somber classical music on the car stereo. Purely random, as I had selected the music for reasons that had nothing to do with the crash. It seemed to fit.

The van and other wreckage were gone. However, the story was written clearly in the bent guardrails, the deep grooves in the median, the spray-painting to mark for the investigators where the van came to rest. I thought about three families, surely good friends, perhaps talking and laughing, sleeping, reading, and then moments of chaos, followed by darkness, pain and panic.

That night I watched the opening ceremonies of the 2008 Summer Olympics in Beijing. I watched the faces of the Japanese team as they marched in the stadium, standing tall, strong, and waving at the nearly 100,000 people in the stands. Nearly three-quarters of a century ago their grandfathers had swarmed through China, murdering and raping in the name of their emperor.

I wondered who else might be among the Japanese athletes if the two A-bombs had not been dropped, what additional grandfathers might be watching proudly from the stands, or on a TV back home. I wondered if, in those powerful physiques might lurk some genetic fluke, arising from radiation that might someday lead to some unknown tweak in the human genome, whether for good or ill.

I blinked and looked back to something I had been reading. Just too random to think about, too complex. No easy answers here.

The creek had been low for the past couple of weeks, but the millions of random drops have brought it back up by a couple of feet. The carp are poking around over bottom that had for a while been dry ground, looking for manna. Heron stood, newly attentive. None ponders the randomness of their fortune, I think. I do, but without much result.

Summer in a Jar

I could not help but note that the man extracting honey from the combs in the Langsroth frames looked almost bearlike, solid and powerful, with dark hair and a great black beard.

"Taste that."

The beekeeper pointed to a dollop of honey on top of a rack of honeycomb frames. Bees marched around it like sentinels.

It was the sort of command that brooks no  argument about hygiene. A worker bee looks on suspiciously, as I wallow my index finger in the liquid and finesse it into my mouth, trying to keep the honey out of my tie.

My tongue felt like my brain does when I have read a good poem. The flavor was both sweet and smoky, like good blues sung by a woman.

"They've started using honey in burn wards, to treat badly burned areas," the bear said. "It is high in nitrogen, and germs can't live in it."

I could believe it. I felt better myself.

It is harvest time in fruit country, at least as far as the beekeepers are concerned. Something there is magical, or at least alchemical, about honey, as though some hoary wizard had found a formula for distilling the fruit blossoms of spring, the heady wildflowers of summer and even the much-maligned goldenrod of late summer into that dark amber liquid, sweet as all the things you think you remember about your first love.

In the air, one can sense the beginning of the end. Not in coolness, though that day had been cool enough to wring the haze from the skies, leaving the tail end of the Blue Ridge rumpled and blue, as advertised, in the west. More in restlessness in the summer air, a new timbre in the drone of the bees, a stirring of northern airs, fall leaving its first calling card.

The sky, all pewter blue, tangerine, peach, silver top-lit clouds almost purple as grapes underneath, showed sharp outlines not seen through the soppy hot air from the tropics.

No, summer is not done, but it has begun to pack its bags.

The beekeeper helped a bee find its way out of my hair, explaining that the worker might be entangled and sting me out of frustration. All in favor of calm bees, I stood still while he coaxed the insect out.

The bee stood on the tip of his calloused finger, resting.

"See how frayed its wings are?" he said, pointing at the nearly transparent v-shaped wings."That is what happens to them. They get where they can't fly anymore."

He tossed the bee into the air, where it seemed to fly uncertainly. It flew back to the group of us, landing on each in turn, as though seeking direction. It was a worker doing field duty, hunting nectar, which meant it was in the last two weeks or so of its six-week life. It suddenly occurred to me that the year that had been rushing by me has been a whole string of lifetimes for the bees in the hive, tattered, working themselves to death, generation after generation, toward the distillation of a season.

The air from the north tossed the trees and stirred the dust. The bee from my hair wobbled through the air in the direction of the hives. I drove slowly home, a jar of dark summer beside me, an eternity of summer beginning to fray in orchard country.

A Failure to get Lost in Space

Lying on the blanket in the hayfield, I found myself getting really irritated with Hollywood.

It was late; way past the time when I would have been asleep if I knew what was good for me. It was one of the nights of the Perseid meteor shower, one of the few that were not overcast, and I had vowed not to miss the whole thing.

Sadly, I have to say it was sort of a disappointment. True, it was not an especially heavy night, meteor-wise. A total of six streaked across the sky during the hour I watched, burned up and gone almost before one could really see them. I was hoping for something more spectacular, regular armadas of flaming stone, flashing across the heavens like, I do not know, battalions of angels at the Last Trump.

I remember ooohing and aaaahing at meteorites when I was a kid. I would imagine some ancient chunk of intergalactic rock caught inexorably in the Earth's gravitational field, arcing in at 50,000 mph or so, bursting into flame, tumbling, flaring, until finally consumed.

Lying there in the field under the curious gaze of the cats and in the hungry care of mosquitoes, it seemed I had lost some of my sense of wonder at those brief and seldom streaks.

Part of it, I suppose, is getting older. Kids do awe really well. They have not learned to be cool about it; act like everything is known, old hat, and run-of-the-mill. I do not know why we are like that, but there it is.

Some of it I blame on Hollywood. After all, once you have sat through computer-generated meteors and asteroids the real thing comes off as tame. Of course, the real things I saw incinerating in the Earth's upper atmosphere were pea- to basketball-sized. If one or two the size of a cruise ship had barreled through, I imagine I would have sat up and taken notice.

Or dived for cover.

To tell the truth, I think the main reason I felt grumpy that night was the simple discovery that lying down on the ground and getting lost in the stars is a lot harder that it used to be. Time was I could lie there for hours, reveling in the streaks of fire, and trying to imagine the unimaginable spaces between the stars.

Now, things intrude. The ground is hard, uneven, and my back complains. The bugs seem to bother me more than I used to. I worry about poison ivy.

The worst part is my mind. It will not shut up. Wondering what time it is, as though that mattered in the grand scheme of things. Making plans, lists, wondering about my future, what to do with it, how much of it there is. Even, God knows why, a chorus of a song I hated long ago, running endlessly around in there.

It was, I thought, like trying to achieve a state of grace or trying to write poetry during a big sale day at some cut-rate discount store, where everything is for sale but there is nothing of any value.

Finally, dutifully, I struggled up off the blanket, folded it up and put it back in the car. I trudged responsibly back to the house, painfully aware of the alarm clock looming in the bedroom, a vengeful god. Within only a few minutes, I was in bed, sleeping.

For all I know, the heavens above me smoked with meteors, and rang like a struck bell as I slept.

Snapper Envy & Totems

\#   In the realm of missed opportunities: As I drove through the battlefield on the way to the post office, I saw a little boy of about three years of age, standing on his tiptoes at the Mississippi memorial, grasping the finger of the slain bronze soldier. No camera. Naturally.

\#   My lineage, as best I can figure, is German, Dutch, Irish, and probably a little Milkman here and there. I have been wondering what totems my various ancestors once had. If I were to have a totem animal, it would surely have to be the heron. They keep popping up in my life, especially around this house. There was one here the day I decided to buy the place. Tonight, as I sat near the stream watching nightfall, one flew almost overhead, croaking quietly to itself, skimming through the trees like a ghost.

Truck

My old truck gets used for chores on the weekends, and not much else.

It is not pretty, but it is always helping me to discover things. In its own funky way, it reminds me to pay attention to things I am usually too busy – and going too fast – to notice.

During the week, the truck sits in a sunny spot by the garage. I have a window screen laid between the dash and seatbacks and am drying peppers and tomatoes in it. They are great seasonings in the depth of winter. As a bonus, the inside of the truck smells great. (See note below.)

The Dakota is a 1987 model, with maybe more than its share of dings, rust, and rattles. It has a v-shaped dent in the top of the tailgate from a time when I was showing off my skill at driving in reverse. It gets lousy gas mileage.

When I was younger, I used to name my vehicles. My old Desoto was Hernando, of course. A '53 Chevy was Fat Albert, a lima-bean-green '54 Plymouth wagon was The Tank, and a Chrysler wagon was Walter, after Walter Cronkite (it is a long story.)

I do not name them anymore, but at the urging of my friend Tristan, who was 12 at the time, The Dakota is now Truck.

When he has been sitting for a while, Truck blows oil smoke like a mosquito fogger for a mile or so before he settles down, so a valve job would be a good idea, but it will have to wait.

Truck has two-wheel drive, nothing fancy, even when it was new. Manual shift, no air-conditioning., a little chrome trim, but not much.

About the only nod to the silly modern habit of sissyfying trucks into odd hybrids of utility and luxury is blue velour upholstery, which now smells of an amalgam of dried peppers, spilled coffee, mildew, and god knows what else. Oh, and insecticide, from last summer, when I discovered that the truck had been parked so long that an ant colony had taken residence on the floor behind the driver's seat.

My neighbors used to kid me about how much manure I hauled in when I started my garden. I explained that I was a newspaper reporter, and so had an endless supply of it, usually supplied during elections.

Honestly, I do not know what I would do without Truck.

Never mind the utility...Truck brought me back in touch with some things I had not realized I was missing.

I noticed it the first summer. I had the windows open as I chugged along a back road on my way somewhere, keeping my speed down to 35 or 40, simply because it was the weekend and I was not going to hurry anywhere.

I drove past a cluster of Sweet Olive shrubs in full bloom and was hit by that knock-you-to-your-knees aroma, like honeysuckle on steroids. It made me realize that as fine as A/C is, it does tend to seal us away from the world.

Like most other things, driving with the windows open in the country can be a mixed blessing. Sure, there are flowers and new-mown hay, burning leaves, somebody grilling steak, rain on the road. There are also the sinus-slapping odors of aged manure being spread over a field, or a week-dead deer, a bloated, furbearing zeppelin, hooves heavenward in the gutter.

And the sounds...the high chirp and trill of a redwing, crunch of tires on gravel, peeping of peepers in the spring and buzz saw singing of cicadas in the summer, the faraway stutter of a John Deere tractor, the sticky hiss of my tires on hot tar, rusty chirr of crickets, whirr of grasshoppers, cries of hawks, and the inelegant gronk of the graceful heron, all punctuated by thunder, the lowing of cattle, and snatches of bird song and squirrels scolding the world.

Sometimes, I will even pull over and shut down the engine, and just listen. Listening is something Truck reminded me to do.

I have used it to haul furniture, fieldstone, gravel, sand, soil, mulch and manure. While hauling manure, I learned that it is good practice to close the truck's back to prevent the cargo from being sucked into the cab. Flying manure was not something I would stand in line to experience again.

And you thought education had to be expensive.

Note: Drying veggies in the truck was an idea I got from artist Val Webb of Mobile, Alabama. She writes The Illustrated Garden blogsite at www.valwebb.com. Check it out.

Wayward Lettuce

August is that time when one looks around and sees all the things that one had meant to do over the long months of summer. I did not know vegetables could grow so fast. Everything was going fine until the deer, groundhogs and rabbits found the garden. In one night, the deer munched their way through a whole row of sunflowers and some of the corn before making their way to the front yard, where they helped themselves to the green pears the squirrels had knocked down....

It is hard to be angry at something that beautiful. Nevertheless, I manage.

We put wooden stakes at six or eight foot intervals around the garden. Atop each one is nailed either a half bar of hand soap, or a sponge soaked in laundry detergent. The deer have since avoided the garden.

The bunnies seemed only interested in the lettuce. That problem we solved by scrounging up a motley collection of old milk crates, bicycle baskets, and metal wire freezer racks, which we placed upside down over each pair of lettuce plants.

It works wonderfully. Every night we go out, lift up a basket, and steal the center part from a head of lettuce. By the time we have been through most of the row, the leaves at the beginning have grown back. It feels like cheating.

The only downside is that it does look a little strange, like a zoo for vegetables, or a detention center for wayward lettuce.

What drives us crazy is that the field to the west of the garden brims over with corn...53 acres of it. The deer steadfastly wade through that vast sea of field corn and try to raid the sweet corn in my garden. I guess I should feel flattered.

And never a word of thanks.

Walking through my garden at the tag end of summer is like looking through an old family album and finding photos of me as infant and toddler, brimming with possibilities. In those old photos, I seem to be asking the question: "what's next?" I think my more recent portraits might look as though the question has changed to "NOW what?"

If photographs are windows to the past, it is probably a good thing that they are made of one-way glass. Come to think of it, while I often take pictures of my garden in spring and early summer, I never do so at this time of year. I might look at them the next spring, and just not bother.

This is the time when the ragged truth is held up to the ideal for comparison: How the morning glories that I should have ripped out mostly overran the beans. How half of the corn came up a little on the puny side, despite the manure and the soaker hose. And how the melons were savaged by turtles.

As for the tomatoes in the raised beds.... Well, there could have been more of them, and they could have been bigger, but they could not have been better.

And the asparagus. Let's just not talk about the asparagus. If my garden was a family, the asparagus would be the weird uncle kept locked in the basement.

Then again, there are all the pleasant surprises. The aforementioned morning glories festooning eight-foot-tall sunflowers, colorful as a Mardi gras float. Fat, luscious cherry tomatoes volunteering almost everywhere. A new climbing bean I would never tried before that succeeded far beyond anything I could have thought.

If you have not figured it out by now, this is also the time when I wonder if I really want to go to all this trouble next year. However, always there is an evening like this one, when I sit in the garden and the whole enterprise once again looks...possible. It may be while I sample a tomato or my teeth snap into a fresh hot pepper. Or even as I observe a praying mantis plot the doom of a fat grasshopper, and watch Marsh Creek flare into an outrageous pink reflection of the twilight clouds.

I stand up in the fading light and watch the weary yellow-green tangle of vine and leaf dissolve into soft shadow, and decide: The garden is an imperfect thing, a work in progress. So am I. The garden and I will forgive one another, and try again next year. I make my way through the railroad ties that enclose the raised beds, stubbing my toe only once.

Bugs and Art

According to the King James Version of the Old Testament's 19th Psalm: "The heavens declare the glory of God, and the firmament shewith his handiwork."

Actually, if you look a little closer, the Old Boy seems to "shew" a quirky side as well.

There was a praying mantis that lived in a potted plant on my back porch at the apartment where I used to live. I appreciated her for a number of reasons, not the least of which was her role as a reminder not to become overly sentimental about "nature."

Most often, when you hear somebody say he enjoys "nature," what he really means is that he enjoys scenery.

"Nature," after all, is the whole package, from the dawn mists around a forest cataract, to the shelled and jointed things humping and dragging their way through the leaf mold. These are what the essayist Loren Eiseley called the "ugly, innocent, necessary" sides of what we toss under the easy heading "nature."

When I lived in town, I often said that I missed Nature. It was an absurd statement, like standing in a forest and saying I longed to see trees.

I do not remember the exact quote, but French naturalist Henri Fabre once said his own back yard contained enough nature to keep him busy for a lifetime. I read somewhere else that the typical suburban yard contains some 40,000 spiders of various sizes and species, and a cubic foot of soil from that same yard may contain billions of individual living creatures.

What all this means, if one lives in town, is that one does not need to look far to find a very busy nature; one need only look more closely. Living in a third-floor apartment surrounded by asphalt and a few plants I grew myself, I lacked even a back yard, but still found plenty of things to watch.

The mantis, for example. She is cousin to grasshoppers, cockroaches, crickets and walking sticks. Like other insects, she has just enough brain to operate her angular body and that is about it. Insects are hard-wired, operating on instinct, each species mass-produced by nature from a single mold.

I once saw a spider trying to salvage her web during a powerful storm, mooring one of the stays near the spot where the mantis poised, all patience and severity. In the morning, the abandoned web fluttered in the light breeze.

The mantis, calligraphy against white boards, eyed me as I walked past, her strange, triangular head pivoting on its ball-and-socket neck.

One night I watched as she ate another mantis. While it is true that the female usually eats its mate, I do not think this was the case. The unfortunate Romeo usually gets his head eaten off during the mating, possibly to prevent him from changing his mind. This victim still had its head.

This mantis lay horizontally before "my" mantis, clutched in the spiked front legs, being eaten aft to fore. Horribly, the victim continued to gaze about, only mildly interested in the proceedings, its antennae waving a vague semaphore while the clockwork mouthparts of its destroyer munched away.

These are the kinds of things that can get into your dreams at night and make you twitch. The profligacy of insects is necessary but the stuff of pure nightmare. If predation and sheer accident did not kill most of the young who wriggle near the bottom of the food chain, we would be wading through seas of the things in a matter of weeks. The clattering females of the thousands of species must lay eggs by the tens of thousands in order to keep ahead of the mortality curve.

The same day I watched the little act of mantis cannibalism, I watched two dragonflies trying to lay their eggs in the parking lot out back. Female dragonflies lay their eggs by dipping their tails into the water of ponds and streams.

The dragonfly in flight is a spectacle worth watching; perhaps nothing else in the insect world is so graceful or so swift. Edwin Way Teale, who called them "winged bullets," said some species could achieve speeds approaching 60 miles per hour. The largest living species reach wingspans of seven inches. Fossilized dragonflies with wingspans of 30 inches have been found.

The dragonflies are almost wholly creatures of the air. They scoop their prey into their clustered legs and eat literally on the wing, letting the drained bodies fall without missing a wing beat.

For all their grace, they are not bright. The dragonflies in the parking lot were trying to lay their eggs on the shiny roofs of automobiles. In the smaller species, males fly coupled to the female, who are too small to break back through the surface tension of the water after they lay their eggs: the males help pull them up again. In this case, the busy couple flew from car to car, thudding uselessly against the shimmering surfaces.

I sometimes watch this kind of thing for hours, on walks in the woods or along a pond, until I just cannot watch any more, and hockey-mask faces and Rube Goldberg movements haunt my uneasy sleep.

But even so, I go back, ever curious for more. If I have learned anything in my somewhat spotty education, it is that nature, like art, is a process, not a done deal. More importantly, as in art, one cannot begin to learn from it until one casts aside any expectations that it is going to be pretty.

Cicada Killer

The wasp sounded like a WWII medium bomber, making runs over my desk and my nervous head.

My usual policy toward critters is one of detente; having grown up guilty of the usual atrocities committed by small boys, I try to make amends by not killing anything simply because it annoys me.

I admit that I am somewhat flexible with that rule if the critter in question is of a category that bites, stings, or causes evil smells.

Wasps make that second list, no problem.

This was a cicada killer, a yellow and black beast nearly an inch-and-a-half long, dramatically patterned in yellow and a rich chocolate brown.

I was trying to concentrate on writing a news story, while this giant wasp bumbled around my office. She could not find her way out, and she seemed to be getting irritated.

Then, she flew into the ceiling fan, which batted her across the room into the wall. This did not improve her mood at all.

She dashed across the room another time, right back into the fan. This was beginning to look like one of the Three Stooges movies. The second swat from the fan REALLY ticked her off. She was beginning to fly with an attitude. It is hard to explain, and may have been largely my own apprehension.

Just to be safe, I swatted her.

Later, when I had finished my story and transmitted it, I put the wasp under a strong light and looked her over with a magnifying glass. Wasps are one of those creatures I have always thought the most intriguing in their "design."

With its striking color patterns and sleek shape, she looked very much like what she was, an efficient and dangerous predator. I am very happy they are small.

The writers of horror stories would do well to study the insect world for a source of inspiration. I have not yet seen a horror film that managed to set me to shuddering as much as the day years ago that I was looking at a dragonfly's head under a microscope.

The animal had just molted out of its pupal stage in an aquarium in my living room (did I mention I was still single?) and was getting ready to fly. I had been watching it for some time, waiting to see it take off. It buzzed its wings a few times, and then seemed to run down, like a clock winding down.

Finally, I checked. It was dead. Curious, I place the dragonfly under a low-power microscope, to see if I could see anything out of the ordinary. Looking at the head, I noted that the geometric area between the great compound eyes was so black it looked like a hole.

At the same moment, that I realized it was indeed a hole, a tiny worm poked its head out from within the head of the dragonfly, chewing, endlessly chewing. I do not think I even touched the floor on the way out the door.

SEPTEMBER

Gardener at Twilight

The old man tottered slowly across the lawn to the tables set out under a homemade frame covered with a tarp of an uncertain color.

The hand-lettered sign advertised "Sweet Corn," but there was none to be seen. He kept the corn somewhere out of sight.

On the tables, pasteboard boxes displayed zucchini, a half dozen varieties of peppers in green, red, yellow, and orange. Squash and melons, cabbage, all fat and full and blemish-free enough to cause a bright green envy in any gardener.

The gardener was as small as a hickory nut. He was old, like part of the mountain looming behind his house, with a full head of white hair that spent most of its time under a red and white baseball cap. His skin shone pale in the fading light, his eyes rimmed in red.

A square bandage covered part of the mottled purple skin on his left forearm. He moved quickly, with short, rapid steps.

He did not say much. He shook hands and nodded when I gave my name, and mumbled something that might have been his own.

"Is there corn? Is it all gone?"

"I keep it inside. Four dollars the dozen. Want a couple?"

I had four dollars.

He stepped through a break in the barricade of tall yews standing in front of the house.

It was not a typical southern Pennsylvania farmhouse; yellow brick, windows in a Victorian trim, with a Mansard roof. Like him, the place was worn and a little tattered.

I am a gardener, too, but my vegetables rarely come out so handsome.

Weekends are my time in the garden. Sometimes I work my butt off. Sometimes, I just poke around and daydream.

After a while, the old man came back with a dozen ears in a cardboard flat.

"The bag broke, so I put them in this box."

I handed him four singles.

"Beautiful vegetables," I said, thinking to draw him into a conversation. Maybe pry a few secrets out of him.

"Thanks. Been hot today."

No secrets today, then. I smiled and walked back to the car. I stowed the corn behind the passenger seat. As I eased behind the wheel, I saw him standing between the tables, his pale hands glowing on the peppers.

Lost in the Garden

One of my favorite things to do is to lose myself in my garden.

Off to one side of my vegetable garden is a little open area under a cluster of trees, an elm, a couple of sweet gum, and a Sweet Olive bush. The space holds a couple of chaise longues and chairs. Think of it as a sort of den without walls.

It is generally a quiet spot, at the highest point on the lot, with 50 acres of corn or soybeans on one side, and a gentle slope of trees, shrubs and flowers down to the house on the other side.

I make many of my weekend phone calls from up there because the signal is good. Sometimes I go up to read or write.

A sign my dad used to have hanging on his wall said: "Sometimes I sits here and thinks, and sometimes I just sits here."

I have sat so still there in that space that a cardinal once flew over my head so close that the air of his passage stirred my hair.

Late afternoon is best, when the light slants in just so, and the breezes come alive, dancing in with a cargo of whispers from their passage through the crops.

Not surprising that I would sometimes nod off, stretched out on a chaise like that.

The really neat thing is when I first swim back up to consciousness. I am aware of sound, a rustle of wind, cry of a blue jay. I open my eyes to see leaves fluttering, branches waving, maybe clouds scudding by.

For maybe a second, perhaps two, that is all I know. Not my own name. I do not remember that "I" am at all, or even the names of the things I am seeing and hearing. I am just a part of it.

Pretty soon, I recognize things not so much by what they are, but by the labels I have been taught to attach to them. I think "tree." If I were German, it would be "baum," French, "arbre," or Spanish, "arbol." Invented tags that have nothing to do with what the tree, after all, is.

Then it all comes back in a rush. My mind is fogged with labels and details; who I am, what I need to do that day, the feature story I really need to get started on because it is due Thursday, the prescription waiting for me at Gruber's Pharmacy for one of the annoyances of growing older. Growing older itself, which reminds me that there is more time behind me than there is before me. And that someday the leaves will be dancing for somebody else.

I get up, stiffly, and limp off to where I left the lawnmower. There are details to attend.

Poem: Wait!

Here and now,
I wish I could make it all stop,
Just for a while.
The world, I mean.
Time.
Make it stop at this moment,
As this golden glass-sharp light
Slices almost level with the
Ground as the sun nears its setting...
See it cast gold on the
Flanks of geese against the
Half-moon whose twin dances in the
Water outside my window.
If only I could
Raise my hand and
Still the skies and earth,
Spend myself in adoration
Of this very moment.

T.W. Burger

AUTUMN

If you have a garden and a library, you have everything you need. **Marcus Tullius Cicero**

Equinox & Skittish Weather

The weather has been skittish as we near the skirmish line between summer and autumn. Now, the Earth is leaning away from the sun, as though it fears an explosion. Maybe it knows something. Today has been overcast, though the forecast rain has not occurred.

Meanwhile, the garden that seethed with green only a few short weeks ago has begun to brown and crinkle, like paper near flame. Riots of grasshoppers careen and clatter through the raised beds and the wildflower thickets when I walk by.

The caterpillars, those that survived the marauding birds, wasps, spiders and mantises, grew fat and sleepy as the summer passed and eventually became moths and butterflies.

In the garden this afternoon, I stood making a mental ledger of the pluses and minuses so far this year. It was suddenly clear why writers cannot resist using gardens as a metaphor for life. From that standpoint alone, gardening is worth doing.

After all, one tills and sweats and plants in great hope, and reaps, literally, what one sows. That is, one reaps what is not chomped by deer, sucked to desiccation by squash beetles, or withered to nothing before one's eyes for no apparent reason.

I have often written of the garden's drama, of its ugly and necessary cycle of eat-and-be-eaten; it is a sun-dappled stage, on which all the players are eventually devoured, from aphid to microbe, from mantis to, in the larger sense, me. Eaten by each other, eaten by disease, or eaten by time, it all comes down to the same thing in the end. The garden of eaten.

So, now and then I take stock. Now, the corn is gone. The black-eyed peas and baby limas I did not eat fresh are ready to be picked, shelled and put away for later. The zucchini continues to yield gamely but, as happens every summer, the appeal of zucchinis wore off long before the plants stopped producing. What does not end up as zucchini bread winds up as compost.

In my garden, the tomatoes are the stars, German Johnsons the size of softballs, red as blood and meaty, sweet as berries and almost seedless. Cherry tomatoes that volunteer every year near the compost pile explode with flavor when one bites down on them. I have not given away many tomatoes. Zucchinis, yes. Tomatoes, no. Call me greedy.

On the down side, none of the early peas did well, and the potato beds were a joke. The acorn and banana squash plants fell victim to brownish gray swarms of squash beetles, a noxious beast that seems to have no natural enemies beyond the bottoms of my shoes.

It is ironic that the okra, which I planted as an afterthought in a section of what used to be the gravel driveway, has flourished better than most of my more pampered vegetables. Perhaps, if I am going to insist on making my garden seem symbolic of something, that very fact may not be a bad one to call attention to.

As for me, well, like the garden, results are mixed and not all precincts yet heard from. Not that I kid myself. I will show up for a few springs yet, stir the dirt, annoy the assorted pests a little, and then be gone, tick to tock.

There will be other gardens, other gardeners. If I have learned anything at all in my few years between the rows, it is that there will always be another spring, a chance to take spade to winter's wreckage and till in something new.

Squash beetles, paltry peas and all, in my mind I am already tilling under the mistakes of this year, a brand new garden, lush and weed-free, taking shape in my imagination.

That may be the best metaphor of all.

Bathing by the Creek,

The last two nights were quite cool, the air so clear that the sky seemed a thing of black glass.

Yesterday morning was cool enough for a sweater, though by afternoon one would have been unbearable.

Standing on the deck tonight, something took me back to the first fall we lived here, before the deck was built, when we were first remodeling parts of the house, the shower in particular.

We had been bathing in the back yard for some weeks.

Sue had been tiling the wooden shower surround I built, and said we would need about a week to allow the tile grout to cure. Overall, it turned out to take a good bit longer.

Anyway, summer was done. Nights when we could bear to bathe comfortably under the moonlight were becoming rare. The night previous to the one I was thinking about, I had stood there steaming in the moonlight, looking rather like some clerical functionary from the back office of Hell.

Our routine was pretty much the same every night. I would take jugs filled with warm water down the back steps to the back patio, where we stripped, wet ourselves, washed, rinsed, and dried, all under the splendid open sky. Hopefully, away from prying eyes.

We usually did all this at 11:30 p.m. or later.

As we bathed, we could hear the moon goose cry. Every night he waited in the shallows in the middle of the creek bed, honking plaintively every few minutes.

One night the moon, only three days past full, shone down brightly, and as we bathed and he serenaded us.

Done at last, I dried and dressed, and climbed the steps to the back room, and grabbed a pair of binoculars.

There he was. What had been an indistinct blur to my naked eyes sharpened to show him standing still as stone. In the moonlight, he seemed whiter than he was by day. But then, many things seem larger, or more mysterious, or more poetic under that mystic and forgiving light.

He cried out again, and moved his head. The hairs on my arm stirred. Suddenly, I was very aware that I am descended from creatures that retreated to the higher branches at night. Not that I felt threatened physically, not by a goose, certainly. It was only the night, and the feeling I will never lose, that there will always be at work in this world puzzles our science will never solve.

OCTOBER

<u>Wet Morning.</u>

I have been sitting a while by an open window, awash in the very cool air, and a little of the rain, listening to the drops sighing on the open water, ticking against the glass.

Down the road, somebody is working on a truck motor, one that has no muffler. The fat, burbling sound is providing the bass line for the concert, a flock of crows in the trees across the creek provides the chorus.

To hear the crows tell it, the performance is a tragedy, German, even Wagnerian, by the sound of it.

But then, it is a cold rain, and they are in it.

Vacation, and Notes from the Coast

I am camped out in a tiny cottage perhaps 50 feet from the waters of a small, working harbor on the midcoast of Maine. I have been coming here on and off for many years. I always keep a journal of thoughts, observations, and notes from things I am reading, even descriptions of what I cook.

There are 10 cottages, all built by their owner, Leonard Osier, between 1950 and 1966. Leonard is still with us, and in his 90s. He lives in a house painted a good, strong red perched at the top of a hill that slopes down to the harbor, its brood of cabins between it and the water. The cottages are simple wooden affairs with no insulation or fancy accoutrements, but comfortable.

We come here at the end of every season, after kids are back in school and before the "leaf peeper" tourists make the roads a game of Russian roulette as they gawk their way down every road.

We spend a lot of time writing and reading, gazing out the windows – at high tide, we are only about 30 feet from the water's edge – watching preparations for winter.

The owners of the pleasure boats lash their dinghies upside down on the decks, and motor away to have their craft stored out of the water, many of them bundled in shrink-wrap for the season. Crews come in, take the floating docks from the ends of the pleasure piers, and push them to a ramp on the other side of the harbor, where they are stacked over the winter, high and dry.

When we leave after our two weeks, the owner's crew will come in, disconnect the electric, leave the refrigerator standing open, and drain the water from the pipes. By mid-October, all will be quiet, the harbor home only to the boats of lobstermen.

The following is from my journals....

Between two and three a.m., I awoke briefly, and went out on the porch to see what the world was up to.

Spectacular stuff, as it turned out. Funny thing about the world: It apparently has no ego, and will do the most spectacular things while nobody is watching.

The cloudiness that had teased the sky late the evening before had disappeared, leaving the sky clear, the stars bright, even through the thin arm of the fog we had seen offshore at sunset, which had crept ashore while we slept.

The moon we had watched for in vain last night had appeared, though I could not see the waning face from where I stood.

The fog played around the resting lobster boats and remaining pleasure craft, and around pilings, and sifted itself through stacked lobster traps on the working dock across from us. The moon illuminated every droplet of vapor in the fog, transforming it into a silver mist, jewelling the entire harbor.

No admission charged. All that is required is that we show up, and take time to see.

Back to the Grind & the Art of Balance

A common addiction among writers is the keeping of daily journals. Some of us are almost religious about it. Mine, however, is very spotty. Even so, going back through journal entries from years back is intriguing, a sort of personal archaeology, a search for the fossils of who I was, five, 10, as far back as 16 years ago.

Or as close as last weekend.

Sometimes, when bad things happen to other people, I like to look back to see if I was having a good time when I was the same age the victim was when the bad thing happened to him. I think it is a way of letting myself know what a near miss I had.

"See," I seem to say to myself. "That could have been you. You were lucky."

Last Thursday I sat tensely here in my office monitoring the progress of a major hurricane, calling up weather maps and reports through my computer, trying to anticipate whether or not we were going to get damp or drowned.

"I have been on the fringes of several hurricanes now, including Camille (on August 17, 1969,) when I lived in Mississippi," I wrote in the journal. "Despite that real-world experience, the image my mind always conjures up when I hear about hurricanes coming ashore is that of Grendel bursting through the doors of Hrothgar's hall...People in Florida probably feel as though they've done a couple of turns on the dance floor with the old monster himself."

196

The next day I would write a story about the death of a 10-month-old boy, and how the police were treating his death the previous day as "suspicious."

Taking a break on Saturday, I visited friends in D.C. After dinner and a long talk, I went up to my room to write in the journal.

"A hot night, here in the suburbs of Washington. The hurricane brought with her a mass of warm, moist air from the Gulf of Mexico. In her hurry to get to the Upper Midwest and Canada, she left it behind, along with a full moon in a buttermilk sky, several inches of rain and a washed and wind-battered world," I wrote.

That same day, back here, a woman was charged in the death of the baby.

I came home today after a fruitless afternoon chasing a story that apparently does not want to be written. Tossing the briefcase down on the desk, I grabbed the binoculars and walked out to the creek side to see if I could clear the ugly rubble from my head.

An osprey preened itself in a dead tree directly across from me. Shortly after I found a comfortable perch from which to watch him, a blue heron flew upstream, wingtips teasing the water, and landed in the shoals between the fish hawk and me.

I watched them for a solid hour as they performed what naturalist Loren Eiseley called the "ugly, innocent, necessary" rituals of nature. I have yet to see the osprey catch a fish, and I did not today. Apparently he was more interested in looking good than in performing.

The heron rendered his slow deadly dance on the rocks below the dead tree, with startling bursts of motion, thinning the rippling swarms of fry in the riffles between the boulders.

As the light grew dim, I peeled myself out of the chair. The osprey and heron rowed through the air upstream and out of sight. I went in, ate supper, and sat down in front of the computer. First up, charges filed that day against an area couple, one charged with raping the other, who was charged with shooting him.

I took a swallow from the giant coffee mug, and glanced ruefully out the window, where the last of the light played along the surface of the creek. I opened my notes and began typing. Balance is everything.

Carrot Cake at the OK Corral.

The issue of the carrot cakes came up during the usual rattle of gunfire where my mother gets her hair done.

My mother still lives in Georgia, in the bustling university town where I grew up. She likes to get her hair done by Judy, who runs a beauty shop out of her home in the country.

Judy loves birds, and has a number of feeders out in the yard. She hates squirrels, who regularly conduct raids on the feeders, despite the risk of sudden death from the .22 rifle Judy keeps propped up by the door in her shop.

A word to my more urbanized readers who are reacting with nervousness at the idea of a beauty shop operator having a loaded gun at the ready right in her shop. Understand that we in rural areas have a very different relationship with firearms than do city folks. While we do have our Rambo wannabes, for the most part country folk see guns as tools, mostly for hunting and perhaps a little bit for protection.

A few years ago, when I worked as the sole reporter in a newspaper bureau in a small town near Harrisburg, Pa., a woman called me to say her son had found a shotgun shell in the parking lot outside the local middle school. She wanted to know if I intended to do a story about it. I said no, because it was hunting season. It would have been different if her son had seen a student walking into the school with a shotgun. Tragedies like the shootings at Columbine and other places notwithstanding, I think people over-react to the presence of firearms.

I will get to the carrot cake in a moment.

Back at Judy's beauty shop, it is a regular occurrence that Judy will drop everything in the middle of a trim and set, grab the rifle, open the door, and blow one of the little rodents into that big pecan orchard in the sky.

"Lord, I hate squirrels," she typically says, leaning the gun back against the door. Mom says these interruptions with gunfire make her nervous, but she keeps going back because Judy is such a good friend, and anyway she does nice work.

"Anyway, where was I? Oh, yeah," Judy said, resuming her place behind the chair, where Mom sat, watching through the window as the squirrel twitched its last. "I just decided I had enough with Leon and the carrot cake."

Leon was Judy's husband. Since she'd met him some years ago, he'd let there be no doubt that his favorite thing in the world to eat was carrot cake, a dessert Judy was entirely happy to bake for him.

Trouble is, Leon was real fond of the carrot cake his mama had always served him, and liked his mama's recipe a lot more than he liked Judy's, and was not shy about saying so.

"I had had it with that," Judy said. "So, I called his mama and told her I just had to find out how she made her carrot cake. She told me to come on over, and I did. She took me out in the garage, where they keep this big, upright freezer. She opened it up, and there were six big ole Winn-Dixie carrot

200

cakes, still in their plastic containers, pretty as you please."

Judy's mother-in-law said she had never baked a carrot cake in her life. She just waited until they were on special at the Winn-Dixie, and bought a half -dozen of them at a time.

"'What Leon do not know, do not hurt him,' she told me," Judy said.

Therefore, Judy went out and bought herself a mess of Winn-Dixie's carrot cake, freezing all but one. That same evening, she carved out a big piece and served it to Leon after supper, and sat back to assess the results. Leon dipped out a big bite with his fork, put it in his mouth and started chewing. He closed his eyes, gave out with a windy little sigh, and swallowed.

"Oh, my, but that's good," he said.

He took another bite, and leaned across the table to whisper, even though only the two of them were home.

"And, you know, I believe it is even better than mama's."

Mardi Gras Creek

It is the time for autumn things. Time to pull up the corn stalks in the garden so they will be ready for the shredder.

Time to walk around munching on all the cherry tomatoes that grew better than nearly everything else did in the garden, never mind that every blessed tomato plant was a "volunteer," arising from fruit that fell to the ground last year.

Time to think about turning under the soil, adding manure and compost, "reloading" it for the coming spring.

It is time also to pause in the late afternoon to see how the autumn foliage has begun to paint vivid colors in the usually broody surface of the creek. It is as though an old friend known for her serious demeanor had suddenly showed up at the house wearing a pair of flashy earrings. Then a week later, she shows up wearing something gaudier still.

One knows that within a few more weeks, she will arrive dressed like a Mardi gras float, and all we will be able to do is gape at the wonder of it all.

One's attention turns inward as well, both in terms of getting the house ready for winter, and in terms of getting me ready as well.

Projects for the long winter nights are already in their planning stages. Like a general preparing for a battle, I try to prepare for every eventuality.

Of course, the projects that will crop up needing to be done will take precedence, and most of the items arranged for will still be in the planning stages when spring rolls around. It is just the way things go.

Who knows? This might even be the year I get the pictures hung on the walls, instead of leaning, hidden, on either side of the couch, and in the guest bedroom.

In a few weeks, the garden, now scruffy and disheveled, will be all tucked in, folded over on itself to recharge.

I like to think that as I over-winter, penned in this little cottage full of books, I will actually get to read some of them this year, make some progress on my own book, reload, fertilize, and mulch my own mind.

I know there is a joke lurking in that last statement. You can just keep it to yourselves.

Playing Hooky with Darwin

It was on a drive I do not get to take often enough when I thought about the dancers.

Only a few minutes west of where I live, the road rises up out of the sleepily rolling foothills and serried rows of corn into the Blue Ridge.

In the middle of a busy Monday, the wind battered the windows, rattling them in their frames as though to remind me that the change was upon us.

Other years, I confess, I allowed work to carry me along like a leaf in a rain gutter, so that I looked up eventually from the garden, out to the winter-dulled hills and realized I had ignored autumn.

Not this year, I vowed.

I jumped in Truck and headed west, where the mountains stood like a dam against the afternoon; sitting at home is no place to be on an autumn day.

The gusts tore in from the north, shredding the few clouds. The air tumbled in the plain and bounced off the flanks of the hills, as clear in its new coldness as though just made.

It was as perfect as real days get. On the high road, unpaved in some places, summer was busy being evicted. On a high, saffron hill as the trees tossed in the crisp light, the dancers came back to mind.

It had been only a few days before, at a rally held by a stern religious group. The event was held in support of a Bible camp the group wants to build in our area, despite some opposition by residents of the rural community where the camp would be built.

The sermon given by the guest preacher had been artfully done, leaving one with a renewed and proper wariness that the world can at times turn wicked and things do not seem to be the way they were.

We have been hearing that same sermon for the past several thousand years, in one form or another, and it is just as true now as it ever was.

Before the preacher performed his art, the choir from the high school run by the church sang to get everybody in the mood. They were very good.

Afterward, as I stood outside the building where the rally had been held interviewing some of those who had attended, I noticed the choir members shaking off the tension of performing in front of a roomful of strangers.

They were dancing one of those group dances popular at the time; do not know what it is called.

One of the kids in the group kept saying in a stage whisper, "We're going to get caught, ya'll," but did not stop dancing.

I was told by someone in the crowd that this particular religious group holds dancing to be a sin. I do not know if that is true, but when the older members of the church group began coming down the hall, another choir member ran ahead.

"They're coming!" the boy said, and the dancers, their eyes wide with alarm, scattered like leaves and piled into the waiting bus.

No dancer myself, I had to remark that they did not look particularly sinful, only young. Maybe, in the eyes of their church, that was their sin.

A few days later in the autumn woods, I thought of the dancers again. Perhaps it was the tossing of the trees, which moved as though by joy, not the wind. Humans dance. It seems to be the way of things.

We have probably been dancing since our feet touched the ground, whether we were handed down to that ground by the creating hands of God or climbed down there ourselves out of a tree in some dim Darwinian past.

The day was so gorgeous, I almost felt like dancing myself. The moment passed, as the day was passing, a crystalline thing hanging there in the heavens as my part of the world spun away at the speed of a jet liner.

As the sun ducked behind the now blue bulk of the mountains, I stopped at a roadside stand and bought a sack full of wind-chilled apples. I bit into one as I climbed back into the car. It was sweet, with just an edge of tartness.

Back to work.

It is Always Something

"You want a heart?" my neighbor said this morning as I was walking toward my car to leave for the office.

He was walking toward me, his right hand outstretched and bloody, a heart clenched in his fingers.

There was a giddy moment when I thought he had had some freakish accident while chopping wood and was asking for help. Then I ran my mind back over what he had said and realized he had asked if I wanted a deer heart to eat. I believe they are considered delicacies. I have doubts that I will ever find out why.

The doe hung upside-down from a frame in Danny's yard near his tool shed. She was already skinned - around here, they say "skunt" - gutted and washed out. He had pulled her hide down so that it hung inside out down over her head, like a woman peeling out of a tight dress. It looked, well, immodest.

She was well muscled with a fair amount of fat over the top of the meat.

Danny said that when they have a lot of fat, that means a hard winter ahead. I suggested that a lot of fat more likely meant a good food supply over the summer and not a lot of stress running from predators. He dismissed such heresy with a sniff, blowing cigarette smoke through his nose.

I thought I would point out that I have about 80 pounds of fat on me beyond what is absolutely necessary. Perhaps we have a hell of a winter coming on. I thought better of it, and kept quiet. Who am I to challenge conventional wisdom? It is been that sort of week. I should have known that things were going to be a little weird after we spent an evening combing the house looking for the snapping turtle.

There is a great, grim old snapper that lives on the bottom of the creek, not 30 feet from the edge of my deck. It is the prime reason there are not more ducks or geese in that part of the creek. In the spring, when the young waterfowl first begin trailing along the creek surface behind their parents, it is the snapper that preys on the feathery flotilla.

By early summer, only a few remain. I do not know if the snapper takes all of them, but it is big, probably two feet or more, from snout to tail tip. It takes a lot of meat to build a turtle that big.

The turtle in the house is not that big. At least, not yet.

It showed up in the kitchen, a little black spot smaller than a quarter. I picked it up. It was a snapping turtle. I have no idea how it got into the kitchen.

As a boy, I was forever finding wild critters on my hikes through the Georgia woods and bringing them home with me. Inevitably, they either all died or escaped. Among the former were any number of baby possums, some newts, salamanders and toads. Among the latter were some lizards and a really fine black snake. One of the salamanders actually belonged to both groups. He got out of the terrarium I had so lovingly created for him, the ingrate, and disappeared.

Some months later, during one of those Mom-decreed cleanups of my room, I found his little mummified body along the baseboard behind the dresser.

I never found the black snake.

Apparently, I am a slow learner. Now, 50 years later, I found a shallow bowl, furnished it with a couple of flat rocks collected along the Maine coast, an inch of water, and the snapping turtle.

It seemed like a pretty neat place, for a turtle. I had to modify the design with a plastic cover after one of the kittens developed too keen an interest in the snapper.

A few days later, I found the bowl empty, the plastic cover evidently shouldered aside by Arnold Turtlenegger. The little beast was gone.

OK, sure he was small. But the idea of walking around barefoot - I hate wearing shoes, and avoid it whenever I can - in a house inhabited by a snapping turtle of any size was a little unnerving. I spent most of the evening meandering from room to room, bent double at the waist, squinting at the floor, trying to spot the jagged shell of this minuscule reptile among the squiggles and swirls of my oriental carpets.

No luck.

I spent a couple of edgy days, walking gingerly. I wondered how long a small snapping turtle could survive in the dark recesses of my house. More, I wondered how BIG a small snapping turtle would grow, lurking around in those same dark recesses, feeding off, what? Dust bunnies? The little bugs that get into the house despite half an acre of window screens? Kittens? Would I awake in the wee small hours some dark night to hear: Thump! Drag. Thump! Drag. Thump! Drag of a giant snapper finally grown large enough in my home's secret places to come seek his revenge?

Yesterday, I found the baby snapper. He was still of manageable proportions. One of the kittens was playing soccer with him in the sunroom. I retrieved him and plopped him back into his bowl. He is there still, with a heavier arrangement holding the lid on the bowl.

This weekend, I am taking him on a little excursion to a place with nice, clean running water, and lots of little water critters to play with. Only not here. I have enough monsters here, thank you very much. The geese will thank me.

Culprit and the Wooden Heron

It is early morning, and the creek is full of sky. Clearly pewter with a hint of peach, it trembles, snared in a lacing of reflected branches daily more bare as the world tilts inexorably toward the winter solstice.

Every day there is something new to be learned from the creek, if only one takes time to look. Appropriately, today's lesson is one in the difference between looking and seeing.

I stand watching the light grow in the east. The white cat sits on the shelf at one window, staring intently at something. Gauging the angle and direction of his gaze, I try to see what might be so interesting.

On the opposite bank, I make out a lighter area among the leaves and weeds. It could be the neck of a large bird. I grab the binoculars and tweak the focus. It is only a piece of jetsam from the storm last weekend.

"That's not likely to make very good game," I think toward the cat, Culprit by name. "You can watch it all day and it won't move."

The cat gives me The Look cats reserve for humans. Cats, I have always suspected, view us with a certain mixture of pity and alarm. Giving up on me totally, he looks back through the window, ducking his head a little, the way he does when something he is watching moves.

I look back. Nothing. The stick remains firmly in place. I look again through the binoculars. Still just a stick. I look back at the cat, then back at the creek. While I had looked away, some great movement had occurred in the water, for the sky creek quaked and shimmered.

I look back at the cat. No change; still that intense stare.

Back to the lenses. Still nothing but that pale stick, slightly curved, that I had mistaken for a bird's neck.

"One of us is crazy, stupid or blind," I think again toward the cat. His look told me which of us he thought that might be. He stared back across the creek. Once more, I raise the lenses, and almost jump out of my skin at the nearness of the deer.

She stands not 10 feet from the white stick, her neck curved gracefully around to investigate a sound or smell off behind her right shoulder. Expecting to see the nonexistent bird, I had failed to see the very real deer which the cat, who presumably had no expectations, had seen all along.

I look over at him. He did not seem to be actually laughing. I look back. The deer is gone, but the sky in the creek heaves and waves, as though Leviathan himself had passed just beneath, and I had turned back to look only moments after his tail had turned the bend.

As I type that last sentence, the first rays of the sun lance through the thinning leaves of the trees along Marsh Creek Road and into my office. This seems to be a morning in which things will happen only if I do not watch them.

No, that is not quite true. For, as I look at the colors the sun fans into flame in the trees, two large flocks of Canada geese clamor overhead, turned to gold in the dawn light. It is the sort of sight that makes one forget to breathe.

Exasperated, I grab the binoculars, and go outside, to see what miracles might happen next as the sun works to free itself from the hardwood tangle across the creek. But the exposition was finished, the curtain drawn. One show to a customer. From the outer wall, I look back at the house.

Culprit stares out from his familiar perch in the window. I am not sure, but I think he winked at me.

NOVEMBER

Faves, with Caveats

With great flocks of Canada geese passing back and forth on the creek, gabbling like shoppers on a big sale day; with brown leaves swirling like the last thoughts before sleep; with the smoke of neighbors burning leaves and garden waste a pungent incense in the sharp air; with the bright-yet-somber color of the trees glowing like fire in Marsh Creek, its morning mists rising toward the sun as though in homage; with all this, I plant myself squarely on the creek's edge and proclaim this my very favorite season of all.

I do so ignoring the small voice in the back of my memory reminding me that I said more or less the same thing last spring, as the world shook off its long winter slumber and got busy.

I really meant it. Both times.

A little while ago, I pulled a chair up to the deck railing and just sat there in the chill, watching the autumn night and the moonrise fat and full over the old ball ground on the flats across the creek.

It was a very autumnal scene, the water black as space, yet bright enough to send back shimmered etchings of the bank-side trees, nearly naked now. The narrow strip of flat land along the creek and the bank above are a carpet of rich red-brown oak leaves, the brittle stems of summer's daylilies and mallow little but memory.

Everything moves as though it is late for an appointment. Leaves swoop and stir. The squirrels, always kinetic, are more so. The cats, perhaps a bit too pampered, ignore the squirrels, and attack instead leaves skittering across the deck.

It has been a week since I have seen any of the three herons who stalk the shallows here in warmer weather. They are gone, following the sun south as my part of the world leans away, arcing through space and toward winter.

It will soon be time to go in for supper. Just as well. The brisk air has more of an edge to it now. However, I stay a while longer, soaking it all in, trying to memorize sight and sound, knowing it is hopeless, trying anyway.

If more than half a hundred autumns have taught me anything, it is that the brevity of these moments is part of what makes them treasures, and if they could be kept, they would somehow fade even faster.

The Canadas

In his "Book of Days," Hal Borland reports that Canada geese - indeed all birds - have excellent weather sense, "since they are natural barometers - their bones are hollow, and react to atmospheric pressure."

He said he had known flocks to pass up "two or three of what appeared to me clear-cut weather warnings in the autumn, then take off for the South just twelve hours before the season's first winter storm struck."

The birds are also terrific fliers, the former New York Times columnist added, reporting that one flock traveled nonstop from James Bay, Canada, 1,700 miles in 60 hours.

Adventure with The Whistle Pig

It had not been that odd a day, really. Nothing that would have prepared me for such an event, anyway. A couple of interviews, some conversations at the post office about the upcoming elections, and then a trip through the battlefield in time to be back at my office in time for a staff "teleconference."

Driving along West Confederate in the Gettysburg National Military Park, I noticed a woman walking her dog. She was having a devil of a time holding the little black and white cocker spaniel back.

Thinking the dog may have sniffed out a wounded or dead deer, I stopped.

It was a groundhog, or woodchuck, if you prefer, or even "whistle pig," as they are called in Appalachia. This one was not acting right. He walked along, looking bewildered, as though he were a little drunk and not sure what to do next. I snapped a picture or two, and decided to walk along with him for a while.

He would have none of it. He kept stopping, backing up, and walking slowly in circles, all at a distance of no more than three to five feet. I got on the cell phone and called the National Park Service office, asking them to send a ranger, as I thought the little guy might have rabies.

Having done that, I went back to keeping tabs on the groundhog. He had wandered out onto the road, and managed to tie up traffic for a few minutes. I walked over and did what I could to encourage him to get off the roadway.

"Run over the S.O.B," I heard one driver say. I think he was referring to the rodent.

Finally, the little fellow found his way to the berm, and waddled off into the woods. My thought was that I could keep up with him and flag down the park ranger when he or she arrived.

Half an hour later, the groundhog and I had reached a kind of truce. I leaned against a tree and watched him. He hunkered down in some leaves and snacked on a nut, eyeing me with grave suspicion.

A young 'whistle pig" looks apprehensive, moments after he sprung one of my "Have-A-Heart" traps. No more of my leafy greens for him: I released him in the wild, despite neighbors' admonitions that I should eat him.

We had reached a certain amount of detente a little earlier when he, supposedly fed up with this lug tailing him noisily through the woods, calmly trundled up and grabbed my trouser cuff in his jaws, as though hoping to topple me. Maybe he had designs on ripping my throat out.

Anyway, he circled me a few times, not growling, but only, well, confused, like an actor who has forgotten where he is supposed to stand. Finally, as I continued to follow him, he turned walked quietly up to me once more and bit my shoe. Hard. I could feel his muscles straining.

This was too much.

"Look, furball," I said, "you weigh three pounds, I weigh 300. Think about it. This could take a while."

He shook my foot, then disdainfully dropped it and trundled off toward the leaves where he found the nut. (OK: the other nut.) From the back, he resembled some haughty dowager walking away from some rude street corner lout with whom she had exchanged insults.

I looked at my watch. My choices were to continue babysitting a possibly rabid groundhog, or to make it to my staff meeting. Not an easy choice, considering how I feel about staff meetings. I looked at my watch again. Still no ranger. The groundhog offered no suggestions. I walked back through the woods to my car. The groundhog continued to gnaw at the nut.

I started the car and drove off. "Nobody is going to believe this," I said aloud. I looked at my pants leg.

Groundhog spit.

Other guys have hunting stories. Tales of 10-point bucks, ferocious bears, and impossible shots accomplished while falling out of tree stands.

I get groundhog spit.

Figures.

Maybe I should have my pants stuffed and mounted over my mantle.

The Blue Mote

On Valentine's Day, 1990, astronomer Carl Sagan talked NASA engineers into turning the Voyager I spacecraft around, so it could take a picture of Earth from way out on the rim of our solar system, roughly 4 billion miles away. Sagan later wrote of the resulting photo: "Look again at that dot. That is here. That's home. That is us. On it everyone you love, everyone you know, everyone you ever heard of, every human being who ever was, lived out their lives... [On] a mote of dust suspended in a sunbeam."

I believe that we are biological. Period. I believe we evolved to be what we are in the same way everything else on the planet has. Genetic discoveries in the past half-dozen years have provided maps of the human genome telling us that our entire 6-billion-member human species goes back 7,000 generations to an original population of about 60,000.

That is roughly the number of, say, orangutans remaining in the world today, or, coincidentally, the population of Bayonne, New Jersey. The DNA of any two humans is 99.9 percent identical. This means that people the world over are much more similar than they are different. Most of the differences are cultural.

I believe that we are biological, but I have trouble believing that is ALL we are. It seems wasteful. Everything we become in our lives, great poets, scientists, artists, thinkers, flickers out to nothing when we die? The most ordinary human is a wealth of experience and even wisdom. Does that blink out? Is all of that mere data stored in three pounds of gray Jell-O under a dome of skull? My mind tells me yes.

My heart tells me no.

My heart has always feared the dark. It cannot imagine non-being without quailing in terror, though it ponders its apparent non-being before birth without the least tremor...been there, done that. I find this mysterious. As though a man, used to poverty, finds a dime and then lives in terror of the day he will lose it.

I believe that life is a miracle, though not one necessarily conjured by the action of any outside force. It may be that life, however miraculous, is actually as common as beans out there in the scattered worlds of the cosmos.

Matter is energy, dozing, and all life, as we understand it is a strange dance of carbon, hydrogen, nitrogen, oxygen, potassium and sulfur. I believe that Nature wastes nothing. Matter and energy are really the same things uttered in a different idiom. Death and life, decay and growth, chemicals rising up to a fevered tango only to fall back to dust, all is energy jumping in and out of the shadows. It may mean nothing. It may mean everything.

I believe that our minds are products of our bodies, which are the products of chemical and physical properties. I believe that when I die I am dead, a match burned out. I also believe that I will always act and think as though "I" am separate from, though inextricably linked, to all this bumping, jiggling, wheezing gear in which I travel.

I accept that my understanding of the universe consists of contradictions. I believe that this welter of contradictions is a basic human condition, a balance of opposition necessary to keep us from tipping over. A human that believes truly that they are nothing but a few decades of chemical fizz is a heartless biological automaton. A human that thinks he is the earthly utterance of God, a thing essentially spirit, placed here to have dominion over all things, is a dangerous fool.

At the same time, the idea that life may have no intrinsic truth or morality leaves me feeling hollow and afraid. In fact, I do believe there is intrinsic truth and morality, but I do not know how to articulate that belief. I also find myself liking the idea that there is somebody out there in charge, that this is all for something, all evidence and good sense to the contrary. Moreover, I have a whole list of people whom I would like the Almighty to smite.

I believe that there is much we do not understand. I do not believe in ghosts and the 'spirit' world so popular these days. That is to say, I do not believe in the "supernatural," simply because I believe there is nothing that is outside of nature. I believe that much that has been reported as ghosts, UFOs, mental telepathy, and predictions uttered by your Aunt Hattie's tealeaves, whatever else they may be, are events arising from a natural universe. When the mysteries behind so-called supernatural phenomena are explained, it will be science and reason that explain them, not some reedy whisper from beyond the pale.

I believe that God gave us minds so that we would eventually figure out that he does not exist.

I believe Nature is improvident, and spends itself like a drunken sailor. Profligacy is the rule of thumb. Creatures at the bottom of the food chain rapid-fire their progeny willy-nilly into the world's myriad appetites. We are here, the end product of millions of years of primate evolution. The fundamentalists say "not so." Nature seems to say "Exactly so!"

I believe that the growing movement among fundamentalists and "know-nothings" of every ilk may be the most terrible danger our civilization has faced. Attacks by terror and disease destroy our bodies. Shunning real, demonstrable science, rational thinking, and a sense of history, indeed, turning away knowledge for what is more comfortable, will destroy our souls more surely than could any host of fallen angels.

Peeled Starlings

Winter showed up suddenly over the weekend. One would think that a seasonal order that has been around for millions of years would not hold any surprises, but still, it manages.

I went out of town on business and when I returned, it was winter, or something like it, just like that: Trees bare, lawn swirling with discarded leaves. This morning I found some traces of ice here and there.

Distracted by movement in the neighboring field, I propped myself up on my rake and watched a mass of starlings fidget in the stubble, never settling, never still, then peeling away in their hundreds, like a label being peeled off, into the sky.

They poured into the air, swirled as sugar stirred in tea, then blew through the pin oak and populated the silver maple and elm right in front of me, their song like a chorus of rusty hinges. They filled their bare roost against the bright sun like notes on a Bach concerto. Only for a moment. A small hawk rocketed in just over my head and into the maple, and all the black notes swept away in a panic, leaving the hawk perched alone, eyeing the leaf litter for voles, mice, anything that moved.

It began to snow.

Only a flurry, but a promise, a hint.

I laid the rake in the wheelbarrow and headed back for the mound of mulch in the truck. I, too, had business to finish.

Autumn Pears

The fallen pears lie, brown and mushy from last night's freeze. I rake them into a pile, scoop them into a bucket, and carry them to the compost bin, load after load, layering each bucketful with one of crisp oak leaves, for balance.

The sweet rotten smell makes me wonder, as always, what kind of wine fallen pears would make, or what kind of liqueur. Would it carry into the bottle the dark light of November, or hold onto that sweetness? I like to think so, though I note that before the freeze, the yellow jackets drunk on the mashed and fermented fruit seemed unusually sullen.

The pear tree has been there for some time. It is misshapen, pruned long ago by somebody intoxicated or in the grip of some lunacy. It stands so crooked it must hurt. I have thought many times of removing it, replacing it with something prettier.

I will not, though. The tree seems to have so much, well, heart. Every autumn it throws off pears madly, abundantly, carelessly, like a sailor singing into a stout wind. For all the tree's twisted wood, the pears are sweet, if a little gritty in texture. Squirrels fill the tree in season, fattening them up, and if I get up early enough, I can surprise deer standing in the yard, sneaking a fallen treat before the sun rises.

So, I tidy up around it, and leave its twisted form a gnarled gesture against the sky for another year of defiance, blossoms and fruit.

On some afternoons, I sit in the garden near the compost bins, next to fifty-some acres of cornfield. This time of year, the field lies under the scudding gray clouds, its muddy face stubble where the corn was cut for silage.

Some days, if I sit still enough, buzzards cruise by a little lower than usual, or spiral around, falling through the thermals. I am not an expert on buzzards. It probably has nothing to do with me, but I amuse myself thinking they might be sizing me up, wondering if I am just resting, or really done for.

But this day, I sat still, watching a lone buzzard drift back and forth at the far side of the field. I had just finished filling the compost bin with the last of the season's fruit. The old pear tree stood there, dropping the last of its leaves, snugging itself in for winter, getting ready to light up in the spring with white blossoms, and then pave the grass with more pears than anybody could ever use.

I looked back at the buzzard. Did he seem more hopeful than usual? Sumbitch. If he comes any closer, I am going to bean him with a pear.

Dumb Luck

A different world awaited us one morning last week. Sunny to partly cloudy and just above freezing. Maybe. Indian Summer was definitely over.

From the creekside windows, we saw small ducks of a kind we did not recognize paddling rapidly downstream, in a creek near flood stage. The large oak that had become lodged perpendicular to the current a few weeks ago had been pushed aside. We are becoming like Muslims, Sue said. Every morning we arise and face eastward, paying homage. Except sometimes, I take notes.

A still-vigorous wind kept the newly naked trees in motion. The temperature did not hit 40 all day. It was as though the two seasons finally wrestled it out for the title match last night, with winter coming out on top, pinning autumn two out of three.

The man on The Weather Channel called it a Major East Coast Storm. Does a storm have geography, or a culture? Is it an East Coast storm because of its accent? Are West Coast storms more laid back?

Dinner finished, we settled into the living room. The wind hit 80 in gusts outside, we learned later. We could hear it outside, shaking the house and making sounds like an enraged infant.

Trees fell. The power failed briefly. We commented on the flotilla of southbound mallards who hung around in the creek near the house all day long, grounded. The Audubon book says they winter as far south as Central America and Mexico. All those miles to go, and here they are, socked in at Marsh Creek International.

We remained comfortable in our little wooden cocoon, warm and safe as the thunderstorms threw down snow and the temperature submarined 30 degrees in only a few hours. Outside the small warm light of the cottage, the whole sky was one long scream.

We plugged in a movie and ignored the storm, less in courage than in resignation. After all, what can you do? The world was still here this morning, as were we. If we had been younger, we would not have known how much of that was just dumb luck.

An Accusing Canna

As it usually is in November, I am working outdoors at the last minute because I kept putting the chores off. Typically, the ground is muddy, I fall down a lot, use bad language, and my fingers and face hurt from the cold.

A November day like this is why I only have one Canna lily in my garden. Some years back I was in the middle of a damp, cold day of garden chores and figured that the Canna bulbs could over-winter in the ground. I would just put a couple of feet of mulch on them and they would be fine, considering the previous several winters had been mild.

You guessed it; we had one of the coldest winters in years. The ground turned to iron, deep down, and I lost about 50 cannas. The survivor popped up, all passive-aggressive, in the middle of the zucchinis, undoubtedly to haunt me with the memory of its frozen kin.

Anyway, today as I chopped and dug, I was thinking of summer. Not of those sticky, miserable days when it is hard to breathe, much less do any work. No, I would have dreamed of one of those summer days that only happen a few times in the real season: Clear, not too hot, not too humid, as though Norman Rockwell had conspired with the weatherman to get it right, just this once.

Now, if I could just get that Canna to stop staring at me...

DECEMBER

"Flue" Season

It is one of those odd evenings when the clouds hang low, trapping and amplifying the sounds of the highway a mile away. The haunted air moans with the sound of trucks jamming the long slope of the valley created by the creek, sinking south to Maryland.

Around here, preparations for winter are about complete, perhaps a little late, considering the hurry winter seems to be in this year. Those bulbs that are not wintering under a heap of mulch are mostly washed, dried, and put up in the cellar.

The houseplants that grew so lush outdoors are all huddled in the eastern and southern windows, which the canny builders of this old cottage placed to take the most advantage of the winter sun.

Most of us realize that life is a series of tradeoffs, and we have discovered that winter here is no different. On the one hand, the approach of the solstice has meant earlier nights, and increased visits from the fuel oil man. On the other hand, the winter sun leans way over and pours into the southern windows most of the day, keeping that end of the house warm and cheerful.

The creek, too, has put on its winter face. What was once a nearly solid wall of green on the opposite bank has changed to a deep lacework of bare gray trunks, through which one can see cars traveling down the Marsh Creek Road, and the holiday decorations of a house on the opposite side of the road.

The creek itself has taken on deeper, more somber hues. During a snowstorm a week ago, it grew so dark in contrast to the snow it seemed bottomless. Perhaps it is a failure of my own observation, but I have seen no fish jumping in a long while.

Not that the creek is still. What it lacks in leaping bass it has more than made up for in mallards, which we now have in abundance, as well as a few gadwalls and some others I have not been able to find in my Audubon book. I confess I am new enough to wildlife observing that I can tell you that either a duck is a mallard, or it is not.

The sole major outside chore to be done now is the erecting of several bird feeders. These we have had since buying them last summer, meaning to put them up as soon as we got "caught up," a mostly fictional state of being similar to a state of Grace.

Getting "caught up" is like getting to heaven, and one that I am as likely to reach, so the bird feeders will have to be put up in whatever haphazard fashion we can manage.

After that, there is the matter of adding some extra flue pipe to the chimney, which I am told is too short, though it seems to have served its function for nearly three quarters of a century.

With any luck, we will have the house fully winterized by the spring equinox, at the very latest.

Just Deal With It

Well, here we go again.

We have had another early snowstorm. It was perhaps an inch and all the grocery stores took hits in the bread, milk, egg and toilet paper departments.

The snow came as a punctuation to about a week of temps that stayed on the shady side of freezing, with daily highs averaging about 10 degrees below normal, which put a couple of inches of ice across the top of the creek, and an inch of snow across that.

You do what you have to do.

I spent the afternoon cleaning out the garage, by which I mean re-stacking junk from one place to another – I cannot remember the last time I could actually get my car in there – and moving the lawnmowers into the back of the storage shed and making a space for the snow blower. I got the machine fueled and ran it for a while to make sure everything was kosher, then parked it in its new space, ready to carve its way out when we get our first real snow.

A friend in Fairhope, Alabama reported on Facebook just a couple of days ago that they were having snow, which did give me pause. Snow on the coast of the Gulf of Mexico is a notable event. Farmers in Florida are taking emergency steps to protect their fruit crops, and the wire services are full of photos of fountains frozen in Atlanta and dazed Georgians staggering around in what must feel like every bit of clothing they own, trying to keep warm.

There will be some making wisecracks like "So, where's your Global Warming now?" and similar remarks. A cold spell in December is not proof that the climate is or is not changing. The fact that the polar ice caps have retreated further than they have since they formed a kabillion years ago, is.

Despite snow on the Alabama beaches and fountains frozen in the Peach state, it is, as a climatologist said on CNN recently, only winter, meaning that we should just all get over it and deal.

OK, this cold snap might mean nothing, or it might mean we are in for the worst winter since, well, whenever the last bad one you can remember.

Button up your house; drag out the sweaters and long underwear, and stop acting as if it never happened before. Give some money and clothes to your local shelters so the unlucky do not freeze to death, and maybe have a little more to eat this winter.

As for me, I am going to hunker down and wait for the first real sign of spring....the arrival of the seed catalogues sometime in February.

Lonely Goose

I awoke this morning with the temperature down in the lower 20s, and the surface of the creek iced and snowed over. To look at it, it could be a paved road, or a parking lot.

The geese I heard last night were this morning sunning on the peninsula just upstream, including Moon Goose, who always carries himself as though he is the ruler over all. That impression is illusory, as the flock often takes off with a great commotion, leaving him, flightless, calling disconsolately.

Moon Goose. Final Crescent

The Moon Goose, it seems, has waned.

We have not seen him in weeks. We had a flood, a big one, and when the sky cleared and the wan winter sun arose, he was nowhere to be seen. I walked as far downstream as I could manage, and found not so much as a feather. The creek seems a little vacant without him. We hope he was simply carried downstream, and is now hanging out with a different group of Canadas, somewhere between here and the Chesapeake.

Postscript: Bendiction II

It has been some years since I wrote in my journal about the disappearance of Moon Goose. We still talk about him. On the weekend of Sue's birthday, in mid-April, I was at my desk working on a freelance article, when I saw a flash of white out on the creek. Thinking it was one of our local bald eagles, and thinking wistfully of Moon Goose, I grabbed my camera and walked onto the deck.

A white swan. Impossibly elegant, and alone.

The swan haunted the creek for five days, serene and not made nervous at all by people coming to look at it, or by me snapping its photo.

On the morning of the sixth day, it was gone.

The creek feels transformed, blessed somehow. That is just me, of course, failing to see that the creek is blessed every day. As are we all. Amen.